D1426796

SEMIOTEXT(E) INTERVENTION SERIES

© 2013 by Gerald Raunig

Published by Semiotext(e)
2007 Wilshire Blvd., Suite 427, Los Angeles, CA 90057
www.semiotexte.com

Thanks to John Ebert, Marc Lowenthal and Noura Weddell.

Design: Hedi El Kholti

ISBN: 978-1-58435-116-0
Distributed by The MIT Press, Cambridge, Mass.
and London, England
Printed in the United States of America

Gerald Raunig

Factories of Knowledge

Industries of Creativity

Afterword by Antonio Negri

Translated by Aileen Derieg

semiotext(e)
intervention
series □ 15

Contents

I.

Factories of Knowledge

Streaking and Smoothing Space

1

JOSEPHINE, OR STREAKING
THE TERRITORY

Josephine is one of many, a singularity that can only emerge in the multitude, and in the end, she will "happily lose herself in the numberless throng of the heroes of our people." Josephine is a singer, and the multitude out of which she sings is the mouse folk. Josephine is not a folk singer, she does not sing of the mouse folk, she does not sing *about* the folk, and she does not sing *for* the folk either. From out of the multitude, she constitutes an exception. She represents nothing and no one, and nowhere do we find out more about the content or the motives of her singing.

Kafka's "Josephine the Singer, or The Mouse Folk" is not a tale in the conventional sense. The text, written in March 1924 as Kafka's final work, is free from any continuous narrative. It is not a fable and has no linear plot. Instead, it is a treatise on the relation between multitude and singularity, on the form in which singularity emerges from the multitude and how it falls back into the multitude again. This relation is one that goes beyond that of mice, of animals, indeed of any living creatures at all. Josephine is the instituent machine, in whose singing the collective production of desire for reterritorializing, for gently striating, for streaking space emerges. This is not a reterritorialization that invokes an originary community of protection, not a return to a territory long since constituted—but nor is it a reterritorialization that draws strictly segmented furrows, forms a completely striated space, generates a state apparatus. Instead, it is a gentle streaking of the territory, in the course of which the mouse folk becomes an abstract machine, fabricating singularities, events, machinic relations, and gaining its form from this streaking at the same time.

Kafka explicitly poses the problem of Josephine's singing and the desire for it that extends across all the mouse folk, even to those who oppose Josephine: "What drives the people to make such exertions for Josephine's sake?" There is a strange relationship between the mouse folk in its multitude and the singularity of Josephine, between the lack of musical understanding of the many and her singular virtuosity. Wholly unmusical, the mouse folk cannot understand Josephine's singing in its uncommonness; indeed, they cannot even perceive it. In fact, they cannot even distinguish between the mouse folk's common skill of piping and Josephine's patently extraordinary singing.

Piping is the acoustic expression of mouse folk normality. No one would call it art. The mouse folk pipe away without attaching importance to it, often without even being aware of doing it. Yet Josephine's strength is not even quite sufficient for this conventional piping. In all her efforts, she only manages a piping, "which at most differs a little from the others through being delicate or weak." And yet: "There is no one but is carried away by her singing."

Josephine's singing proves to be small, thin, hoarse, light. Josephine's performance is no strong event, no revolutionary break, no triumphant appearance. Her feeble throat, her frail little voice, "a mere nothing in voice," does not roar in the confidence of battle. Josephine's appearance out of the multitude is a weak event, an almost negative singularity. The mouse folk can barely hear Josephine's singing, "she does not save us and she gives us no strength." No pathos emanates from Josephine, no messianic strength, no great notes. The weak event falls short of the strength of the many.

And yet the force of attraction of the singular becomes evident, a desire in the entire mouse folk, when even the slightest impression arises that Josephine could sing. Even the otherwise so thoughtless piping that accompanies the mouse folk through their everyday life, especially when they are contented—this unconscious piping falls silent when Josephine begins to sing: still as a mouse. Stillness is the music the mouse folk love best. Josephine breaks through this stillness, and she fabricates it at the same time with her singing; "she believes anyhow that she is singing to deaf ears." The very musical incomprehension of the mouse folk seems to be the reason for her enthusiastic following. And yet, this is no unconditional devotion—the anonymous narrator from the mouse folk stresses again and again that the mouse folk never unconditionally capitulate to anyone. It is rather a recurrent collective production of desire that the singing, or even just the imagination of the singing, elicits in the multitude.

If her throat is so feeble, her singing so unheard, how is the mystery of Josephine's impact to be explained? It probably has something to do with the form of living, the specific mode of existence of the multitude, out of which she is singularized. The mouse folk live in dispersion and permanent movement. The mouse folk smooth spaces wherever they go. Deterritorialization is the normality of the mouse folk. They perpetually flee in all directions, just because they see themselves required to do so for economic reasons: "the areas on which, for economic reasons, we have to live in dispersion are too wide" to be able to live a contemplative life in limited surroundings. Yet the economic reasons are only one side; there is also a desire for dispersion and movement that is immanent to the mouse folk. The mouse folk are almost always moving, often for no apparent reason. Scurrying back and forth, streaming, constantly overflowing, the way the mouse folk spring across the boundaries of a community that is tangible and governable, this is marked not only by necessity, but also by a desire for fleeing without need.

Economic necessity and the production of desire for lines of flight form the two sides of the deterritorialization of the mouse folk.

For a multitude so dispersed and moving, however, the question of assembly, condensation, reterritorialization also arises. To begin with, reterritorialization is also a necessity: the necessity of arrangement, necessity of organization, political necessity. But here too, there is a desire that goes beyond the urgent requirement of assembling out of need: "we like to come together, we like to huddle close to each other, especially on an occasion set apart from the main issues preoccupying us." The accidental reason for the mouse folk to assemble—"It is not so much a performance of songs as an assembly of the people"— consists in the imminent performance of the singer.

Josephine is the instituent machine, reason and mechanism of assembling: The indication of "her intention to sing" opens up the reterritorialization of the mouse folk by itself. Just the news *that she wants to sing* is sufficient reason to assemble. Josephine sings "to gather around her this mass of our people who are almost always on the run and scurrying hither and thither for reasons that are often not very clear."

The territory of assembling is by no means always the same place, which has to be reclaimed each time in the same way, a space specified by habit and law, always the same center of the community. It does not even have to be an elevated place that would emphasize the solemnity of the moment: "it need not be a place visible a long way off, any secluded corner pitched on in a moment's caprice will serve as well." The territory is fabricated in the moment of assembling, by the coming together, by the concatenation of multitude and singularity. This concatenation is singular for itself, it is not repeated without difference.

The mouse folk know that there is more of a tendency to opposition from a distance, but Josephine's voice captivates as they come closer. A centripetal, reterritorializing force, which is so weak that its impact first takes hold in direct communication, in huddling close together, in the intensive moment of occupation. Reterritorialization emerges in streaking the territory, in singularities streaking one another, as occupying and constituting condensation and concatenation. Streaking is not brushing smooth, but rather the opposite: drawing streaks in smooth space with a streaking touch. As it is said in the Austrian south: *das Holz streifen*, streaking or touching wood, barking trees, taking the wood on its path, on the way down into the valley, arranging it, putting it info form. Or *das Feld streifen*, streaking of striping the field, drawing rows, covering the field with furrows, but glidingly, with a light, fleeting touch: gently striating the space and the sociality of the multitude arising from itself.

This is the mystery of Josephine, then. But rather than being resolved, this mystery comes as a refrain: deterritorializing—reterritorializing, dispersing—assembling, smoothing the space—streaking the space; not as opposition, but rather as alternation, complementarity, crossover. Josephine's recurrent singing neither demonizes nor denounces one or the other: neither is it deterritorialization as pure imposition of existential insecurity, nor is it reterritorialization only as constraint, reduction and retreat. And at the same time, this refrain also refrains from uncritical affirmation and romanticization, both in terms of deterritorialization as domination-free movement forward into the open, and in relation to reterritorialization as withdrawal into a homey, secure space of protection.

Josephine's refrain projects reterritorialization and deterritorialization not as opposite, but rather as complementary, even simultaneous. It poses the problem of how this complementary movement of deterritorialization and reterritorialization can also be carried out in a self-determined way, as roaming in space and as streaking space. Reterritorialization here means assembly, condensation, intensification, but not as a recourse to familiar territory, a stable community, an originary protection. Although the mouse folk think they are protecting Josephine, "Josephine, that is to say, thinks just the opposite, she believes it is she who protects the people." What is at stake here, though, is not protection, but rather a self-determined form of reterritorialization, newly occupying space and and its striations.

The mouse folk's reterritorialization, in keeping with the weak event of Josephine's singing, seeks to cautiously, gently streak space. There is no brutal structuring, no conquering of a state apparatus, no massive reorganization of smooth space. Their seeking movement queries the how and where of the new space, the privileged places and preconditions of its emergence. It queries the conditions of assembling as temporary concentration, which does not oppose dispersion, but rather supplements it. It questions how to connect smoothing and streaking, how to mutually interweave the fabrication of smooth and streaked spaces.

2

THE UNIVERSITY-FACTORY AS A SITE
OF RETERRITORIALIZATION

Once the factory was the exemplary site of condensation—not only condensing the time and space of production, but also condensing resistance. It was in the place of the exploitation they shared that workers also found the conditions for collectively discussing, assembling and constituting assemblages of resistance. Today, in the setting of the factory of knowledge, in the universities as well as in the diffuse places of dispersed knowledge production, a mode of radically dispersed production is crystallizing, and occupation, strike, spatial and social condensation, to the extent they are not declared completely impossible at all, turn into mysterious and puzzling matters.

Factories of knowledge: fashionable metaphor for the self-proletarization of intellectuals, misinterpretation of ephemeral Marx marginalia, terminological makeshift solution for the situation of precarious knowledge work? There is no doubt that the General Intellect has been increasingly seized by capitalist valorization in recent decades. Knowledge economy, knowledge age, knowledge-based economy, knowledge management, cognitive capitalism—these terms for the current social situation speak volumes. Knowledge becomes a commodity, which is manufactured, fabricated and traded like material commodities. Immaterial flows of know-how and finances, cooperation and coordination, collective forms of the intellect seem to combine in some regions of the world into a tendency to transform modes of production. This tendency could be called cognification, and this is not necessarily coupled with an improvement of working conditions or a substantialization of cognitive labor.

Yet there are equally compelling arguments for caution in relation to generalizing diagnoses of upheaval, as they resonate in the theses of the immaterialization of labor and of cognitive capitalism. First of all, the "new" forms of affective, cognitive and communicative labor are not fundamentally new. Anti-colonial and feminist movements have long pointed out the gendered and racified division of labor, which banishes everything that does not apply to a certain form of materiality and production, even if it massively contributes to value creation, to gray areas outside the measure of perception. Then in Europe, about a quarter of all workers still work in the industrial sector. And finally, the considerable remainder of dirty work does not simply vanish altogether, but is simply out of the sight of neo-colonial "industrial nations" that have increasingly become post-industrial now: entire large factories have been dismantled in Europe in recent decades, "deconstructed" screw by screw, brick by brick, only to be rebuilt again up to ten thousand kilometers further east. Entire sectors have been moving their production sites into ever new territories, in which the production costs can be radically minimized. Entire industries have globalized or situated themselves in other geopolitical contexts, creating a new international division of labor.

This division of labor is by no means to be situated one-sidedly in a paradigm of progress, in which machines increasingly relieve us of heavy labor, and slavery and exploitation are successively abolished. On the contrary, parallel to the rise of the cognitive, labor under slave-like conditions in factories, sweat shops and call centers, child labor and illiteracy are increasing. And this does not occur only in a simple equation that attributes postfordism to the "First World" and fordism or pre-capitalist models of exploitation to the "Third World." Within the framework of the global metropolis, center and periphery are found in the same place.

Similar reserve is called for in light of an overly hasty universalization of the concept of the *fabbrica diffusa* as well. Emerging in the 1970s in Italy, affiliated with the *autonomia* movement and Operaist theory practice, the concept describes the ambivalent process that followed the exodus of the workers from the factory: a movement of dispersion, diversification, diffusion of sites of production and production assemblages, which first became visible and were thematized in Italy in the 1970s. Not only the fordist factory worker becomes *operaio sociale*, a labor force diffused in society, but the factory itself leaks out and over its boundaries.

The *fabbrica diffusa* emerged from resistance and struggles, in the active flight from the factory, partly into different working and living organizations, partly from work itself into non-work. This exodus is understood from the Operaist perspective not as the effect, but as the trigger for widespread capitalist transformations in the last decades of the twentieth century. From the perspective of the organization of the industrial sector, this dispersion meant a shifting and outsourcing, less in the sense of a new international division of labor, but initially more at the regional level in northern Italy: in the emergence of a multitude of smaller production units that supplied the factories or founded autonomous enterprises. Today this "diffuse factory" has undoubtedly gained further significance, when technological innovations bring an extreme dispersion of the means of production with them, when there is talk everywhere of sub- and self-entrepreneurship, of the metropolises as sites of production, of the "city as factory."

Although the leaking, overflowing and unbounding factory may describe a significant social tendency, the point here is to more precisely define, in a kind of counter movement, the concept of the factory, to the extent that its essential quality consists specifically in the aspects of condensation, assembly and reterritorialization. This focus has less to do with today's modes of production; it concentrates instead on the resistance, the social struggles and the political organizing that, along with their deterritorializing forms of flight, exodus and dispersion, also claim procedures of reterritorialization for themselves: new refrains of strike, occupation, self-organization. The tendency of the question is thus less that of what happens when the factory diffuses into the threads of society, but rather of the positions of the economic and social assemblages in which a becoming-factory, a streaking, an occupying reappropriation of the territory is to be observed.

The factory is—Marx already alluded to this in his analysis of the large factory in the nineteenth century— the container of partial machines, their assemblage, not simply a mere accumulation of partial machines, a machine park; it grows into a machinery that is more than the sum of its parts. The concept of machinery indicates exactly this tendency to ascribe a surplus to the machinic assemblage of the factory, a life of its own. This life of its own can be interpreted in the paradigm of the sorcerer's apprentice, in which the factory worker is reduced to a part of a self-moving and self-governing partial machine. If only this paradigm comes into view, the technical apparatuses must be attacked, there must be a luddite battle against the enslavement of human beings under the yoke of the partial machine and the factory machinery.

In machinic thinking, on the other hand, the factory implies a concatenation of human bodies, their intellectuality and sociality, and the technical apparatuses. The "machinery's" independent existence is then less a matter of the technical apparatuses and the factory as a whole becoming independent, and conversely the worker-engineer does not rule over apparatuses gloriously as *homo faber*. The power of movement that seems to move itself consists specifically and exclusively in the relation of the mechanical and intellectual parts of what is now a *social* machine. Instead of the mechanical and human components of the factory being strictly separated, their effect for the production process is to be investigated specifically in the interweaving and interrelating of the components. It is the physical concatenation of bodies and things, the attachment of the body-machines to the technical machines that allows the flows of production and of desire.

This change of perspective also has consequences for the old question of who *serves* whom, machines serving people, or people serving machines. In *Capital* Marx drew a clear line of separation between manufacture and craft, in which the worker takes the tool *into service*, and the factory, in which the worker *serves* the machine. In these two modes of service, opposing relations of subordination contrast with each other: either a dead mechanism as an arrangement of technical apparatuses retains the upper hand, or a living mechanism consisting in the communication and the machinic-social intellect of the workers. If the relation between serving and taking into service has ever existed in this pure dissociation, the division between dead and living partial machines is dissolving. The distinction cannot be maintained consistently for the factory of the nineteenth century, and even less so now in the twenty-first.

Whereas the factory in the classic view meant the hierarchical setting of relations between technical apparatuses and humans and humans with other humans, a machinic approach understands the composition of the factory as a multi-dimensional exchange among bodies, apparatuses and their environments. In this sense, the factory still remains a site of disciplining, exploiting and subjugating living labor, even though not under mechanical components, but rather under the relation of capital. At the same time, however, the factory is also a quasi horizontal site of machinic subservience, linking aspects of government and self-government together. Concepts such as serving, service, subservience take on the full spectrum of their vivid colorations in their different possible connections between human and machine.

It is not until the factory is grasped in its full complexity as an overflowing disciplinary regime as well as a territory of machinic subservience that adequate strategies of resistance, of economic, spatial and social recomposition, condensation and concatenation can be thought of and tried out. Even in the twenty-first century there is a specific resonance in the concept of the factory, a resonance to the territory, to the condensed composition of technical machines, body-machines, social machines, and finally to the potentiality of assembling. Through the definition of the factory as site of reterritorialization, we arrive again at the factories of knowledge. This concerns less the question of a knowledge production that transgresses the university as an old factory of knowledge to become the unbounded raw material of cognitive capitalism, but rather the opposite: the university not simply as site of a transfer of knowledge, but rather as a complex space of the overlapping of the most diverse forms of cognitive, affective, subservient labor; the contemporary, modulating university becomes a possible answer to the search for today's sites of reterritorialization. When greater and greater portions of production are subject to a radical dispersion of their places and times, when more and more professions—contrary to the condensation in the classic factory—follow in the footsteps of the small-holding peasants of the nineteenth century, whose mode of production isolated them from one another, when territories of gathering, assembling, congregating become rare, this is the matrix of a slogan that emerged in the occupation movements of recent years: "What was once the factory is now the university."

But what is the university? It is undoubtedly true that it has always been an institution supporting authorities, if not altogether an institution for exercising and accommodating to subjugation. This applies to the founding phase of the first universities as well as to the era of the formation of the Humboldtian educational ideal. And it probably also applies even to the brief period of time around and after 1968, when there were intensive attempts to transform the university into an emancipatory endeavor. To the extent that this brief phase was not altogether a myth, it is certainly over now, and it is too easy to state that this has to do with the retirement of most of those who were active then, who contributed to a reorganization of education in the 1970s.

It is debatable, whether it was a weakness of the generation of 1968 that they did not ensure a permanence of their struggles, an ongoing instituent practice, an unbroken chain of instituting. However, beyond one-dimensional blaming it is probably more pertinent to consider the transformations of contemporary modes of production as a condition for the emergence of the modulating university, or more generally the fact that the adaptive capacity of capitalism has taken over precisely the central characteristics of these struggles, in order to flexibly immunize and newly position itself.

What we are now confronted with is a global landscape of universities, which cannot be simply classified in identifiable categories such as neoliberal or reactionary. We experience an extremely complex and geopolitically differentiated situation, in which the old invocations of self-administration and autonomy continue to exist, no matter how they are turned, and in which new authoritarianisms emerge. Authoritarian hierarchies can certainly go hand in hand with soft forms of conduct, budget cuts can coexist with particular rewards, stabilizing procedures can be implemented alongside practices of existential and social destabilizing. We cannot understand all these aspects of the transformation of the universities by looking only at the assaults by authorities that come from above and outside. We also have to consider a certain degree of subservient self-government. Particularly from the perspective of self-reforming and self-deforming, however, there is also a strategy of resistance that can be gained, a double form of immanent desertion.

From the experiences around and after 1968, we can learn that resistive modes of subjectivation and struggles are by no means solely reactive, but also productive and inventive. In the 1960s there was resistance *against* the patriarchal, authoritarian and disciplinary university; however, this resistance also implied re-inventing knowledge production. In the paradigm of the modulating university, now almost fifty years later, the inventive component is even stronger, and at the same time, the virulence of resistance arises even more from just this productive component of modulation: if we ourselves and our forms of subjectivation are the source of machinic subservience, if we ourselves contribute to the modulating university through self-discipline and self-government, then lines of flight can also be drawn on the same field of consistency, which do not necessarily have to serve the machines of the knowledge factory *like that*, not *in that way*.

Such a strategy of resistance can be described as a double form of immanent desertion. Desertion here does not refer to cases such as military desertion or to inner withdrawal and retreat from the world. Rather, it concerns defection from a dead-end situation, so that desertion is always an instituent practice as well. First of all, desertion occurs as the development of precarious forms of autonomy *within* the institution, in the development of little monsters that thwart the structures and institutional antagonisms through their obstinacy. These would be micropolitical strategies, such as refusing to pass on institutional pressure from above, at all stages of the institution; awarding credit points for transversal events that transgress the internal logic of the institution; striking against peer reviews and ranked journals, especially on the part of tenured teachers; actively recognizing journals, magazines, newspapers and essays in anthologies that are not peer reviewed and do not belong to any established hierarchy of ranking, but instead try out new forms of sociality in publishing; inventing and defending free spaces for non-conformist thinking and action; and finally reterritorializing the space of the university as a movement of reappropriation, as was experienced in the occupation movements of 2009 and 2010 in wide parts of Europe.

Secondly, desertion also means deterritorializing and reterritorializing knowledge production *outside* the university, drawing a line of flight out of the university and founding alternative formations of knowledge production. Self-organized collectives that test how local and situative knowledge can be produced outside the universities, newspaper projects and other alternative media that propel critical knowledge production, transnational abstract machines, in which exchange about the struggles at the universities becomes part of the struggle itself. At both levels of desertion, we do not have to retreat to a transcendental territory, but can instead immanently start from machinic modes of subjectivation, which affirm, even over-affirm self-government, self-formation, self-control, until the reforming and deforming of the self is upended, new factories are invented and disobedient modes of knowledge production emerge.

3

TWENTY-EIGHT TENDENCIES OF
THE MODULATING UNIVERSITY

We are cogs in the wheel of an increasingly modularized society, and at the same time we modulate ourselves and the world around us. The mode of modulation is both a striating, standardizing, modularizing process and at the same time a permanent movement of remodeling, modulating, re-forming and de-forming the self. The university, too, is a focal point of this dual modulation, for it is a place where time and space are neatly compartmentalized, where ever smaller modules are produced, and where standard systems of measurement are deployed—and yet it is also a place of indivisible, endless, boundless modulating, a place of the appeal to modulate knowledge and the self. This gives rise to new forms of a modulating university, in which social subjugation and machinic subservience, striating reterritorialization and subservient deterritorialization, modularizing and modulating, become intertwined.

Without the least intention of insinuating any kind of homogeneous development, in the following I will compile a list of problematic issues, which can be observed in specific university contexts in diverse and contradictory forms. In enumerating these issues as a cumulative list I do not intend to create the illusion of a totality or a teleology. Certain components of the modulating university may not be found at all in particular local contexts; smaller educational institutions and arts academies still continue to offer free scope for nonconforming thought and activity. Of course, the pointed formulations of these problems as theses are not to be found to the same extent in all regions of the world either. Almost all aspects of modulation feature pivotal points where they can be subversively turned, and especially in the old centers of the European welfare state, the transformations have been relatively slow, non-linear, and ambiguous.

The harsh neoliberal reforms of the Tory government in Great Britain in the years 2010 and 2011 may be interpreted not as a policy aberration, but rather as a provocative move by the political avant-garde, similar to the way Ivy League institutions established franchises in China, India, and the Middle East as the first manifestation of a new, "global" and modulating university. These tendencies are not simply economic developments, but rather a blurring of manifold problematic issues—components of discipline society and control society, economies of affect and desire. Our knowledge of these developments is accrued not just from isolated, increasingly precarious local situations and their hubs of resistance, but also from abstract machines like those of edu-factory, whose discursive webs fostered the following catalogue:

1. The modulating university fabricates a system for measuring and striating all aspects of know-ledge production, ranging from the credit points awarded to students to the "impact factors" and other economic evaluations of faculty, from time-tracking in the centers of administration to that of subcontracted services and security, from the international ranking of the universities themselves to that of the journals relevant to each academic discipline. This system of measure not only promotes rigid measuring, it also reduces, standardizes and hierarchizes what is to be measured.

2. The quantitative evaluation of services is closely related to payment for these services, which is increasingly being shifted to individual students. The introduction of tuition fees and their successive increase has led to a new elitism in education, to a logic of inclusion and exclusion according to economic criteria.

3. Forcing students to incur debt is a proven method of combating students' resistance and inserting them into the system of "life-long learning." Once tuition fees exceed a certain level, the pressure associated with incurring debt not only affects students' choice of program, but also forces them into a system of

quasi-enslavement. They are aware right from the start that by the time they finish studying they will face a mountain of debt, and that only by landing a well-paid job will they have any prospect of paying it off.

4. Students become not only debtors of states and banks, but also stakeholders in the university. They take on the risks of the university as an economic enterprise and are forced to invest in it as well—not only in the general sense, but also in specific areas such as exam fees.

5. The modularization of higher education transforms university study into an extension of school, in which students continue to be regimented and disciplined. The fragmenting of the period of study, from the division of studies into multiple autonomous segments, through the compounded admission and knock-out exams, all the way to the striating of individual seminars make students permanently start over from the beginning and repeatedly call previously acquired certificates into question. The segmented ordering and linearization of study programs are further exacerbated by a loss of intensity, quality and atmosphere of academic supervision.

6. The slogan "job preparation" turns education into vocational training. As a result of the call for the employability of graduates, colleges become more

and more dependent on actors from the business sector, curricula and choices of studies are channeled in the direction of "labor market needs."

7. Permanent surveillance of the students takes the place of self-determined learning. The tools of e-learning turn "in-course evaluation" and the drill of burgeoning time management into exemplary methods of machinic surveillance.

8. The cautious democratization of university structures that took place around and after 1968 is being revoked. Instead of self-administration and co-determination, a pseudo-transparent, top-down system of enforcement is being installed. At the center of this hierarchy is the client-provider relationship between students and faculty which, when combined with the prevailing methods of evaluation, in extreme cases can spawn denunciatory practices and a system of informers in both directions. Behind the smoke-screen of democratization, transparency, and the curtailing of the authority of teaching staff is the birth of a new assemblage—at the same time a post-authoritarian structure and a machinic invocation—which modulates both faculty and students.

9. In some countries, teaching staff used to be granted civil servant status in order to guarantee the autonomy of their teaching. However, the contradiction between autonomy and being a servant of the state

together with the clichéd image of the lazy and self-important government official made it easy to abolish this nexus. The autonomy of universities is once again a topic of debate, but the idea behind it is now a very different one—autonomy in the sense of entrepreneurial freedom. At the same time, bureaucracy is alive and well and nowadays comes armed with all sorts of digital forms ranging from the general research audit through databases of research activities documentation, all the way to audience-based quality assessment.

10. As elitism and excellence are fetishized, a proliferating system of hierarchical distinctions is exacerbated among the teaching staff: at one pole are so-called researchers of excellence, at the other is the mass of precarious knowledge workers whose main job is to engage in mass teaching.

11. Research, too, is subject to rigid measurement and hierarchization. Content is secondary at all stages of the research process. What counts for the university is the external funding fetish, what counts for the funding institutions is the evaluability and measurability of results.

12. The construction of life in the form of an academic resumé increasingly turns into measuring life. Measurement is to be taken quite literally here, for even in the humanities and the liberal arts, more and

more resumé components are evaluated in purely quantitative terms. At the same time, the biography itself has to modulate, reflecting an uninterrupted, continuous transformation of life or at least simulating this modulation.

13. Wild and transversal writing is tamed and fed into the creativity-destroying apparatuses of disciplining institutions as early as possible. Here, students are instructed in the splendid art of how to write a scientific article, how, in other words, to squeeze the last vestiges of their powers of invention into the straitjacket of the essay industry.

14. In the norming of academic writing, the requirement of methodological self-reflection is preeminent. Before the writers can proceed to any kind of content, let alone political positioning, they practice subjecting themselves to the fetish of method.

15. The chief means for taming wild writing is the academic journal, particularly in its peer-reviewed form. Originally introduced as a way of enhancing objectivity, the peer review has long since become an instrument of (self-)government, and as such bolsters existing structures and encourages their system of inclusion and exclusion.

16. The hegemony of English-language journals has brought about a crass uniformity in the languages in

which academics can publish. This tendency contributes to reducing modes of expression, forms of writing and styles.

17. The dominance of preeminent journals also has a monopolizing effect on the question of authors' rights. Rather than promoting copyleft, Creative Commons and commons in general, journals, institutions and publishers increasingly demand the total relinquishment of authors' rights.

18. The application of business criteria has led to educational institutions being perceived as commercial enterprises rather than as providers and producers of education. This kind of thinking has spawned service agreements, timekeeping systems, benchmarking, monitoring and quality management.

19. At the same time, target agreements, the constant focus on achieving statistical values, and plan specifications at every level lead to an inflexible apparatus, in which the power of invention is not only not fostered, but even implicitly repressed.

20. Although cognitive labor is a key resource of contemporary valorization, knowledge production is actually becoming increasingly precarious. In the extreme case of the outsourced knowledge worker, teaching staff are forced to become entrepreneurs working on the margins of the university enterprise.

21. Assessments of study programs in terms of their market value have become crucial, and not only for indebted students and university institutions. Among educational policymakers who denounce basic research and arts and humanities as "basket-weaving" fields of study and reduce public funding for them, a system of logic is taking hold that rewards "marketable" applied research, especially in the natural sciences, while leaving everything else to the mercy of "market forces" and their social stratifications.

22. The Bologna reform, conceived with a view to making the European education market more competitive, has produced some paradoxical effects, particularly with respect to mobility. It functions as a means of spreading worst practices and has even had a negative effect on education policies in the USA, for example by inducing American universities to shorten their bachelor's degree programs to bring them into line with Europe's three-year model.

23. External accreditation and evaluation agencies, organization and business consultancies are enjoying a growing significance, which increasingly constrains the self-determination of the university in terms of content, especially in relation to future structural decisions.

24. Parallel to budget cuts and the "withdrawal of the state" from education policy, the influence of

sponsors, corporations, and foundations on the universities has increased. While this development is being sold as greater autonomy for the universities, it is in fact leading to their heteronomization and corporatization, in other words, to the direct intervention of non-academic actors from business and politics, as well as to the corporate branding of universities in the names conferred on endowment-funded professorships, seminar rooms, or even whole institutes.

25. The "withdrawal" of the state is not in fact a withdrawal at all, but is actualized in the steering and controlling of the process of the economization of the universities. The university itself is thus becoming diffuse: its relevance applies not only to the terrain of education policy, but also to the terrain of other fields in which politics and economics intermingle.

26. The university is becoming an actor in the intertwined strategies of the real estate market and infrastructure policy: the upgrading of city districts, gentrification, and the transformation of formerly industrial or working-class neighborhoods into zones occupied by the creative economy have become functions of university management. This logic of real estate exploitation leads to the grotesque situation within the university that room rent for universities events is billed internally, that the capacity utilization of office space and seminar rooms becomes a central steering element, that the

system of space shortage results in a new quality of subservient deterritorialization.

27. Competition in the international market for tuition fees has opened up an additional source of revenue, above all for Anglophone educational institutions. Cultural exchanges are used as a cover to recruit students who promise to bring in even higher revenues than the local student clientele. Those who cannot afford these higher tuition fees continue to be increasingly subjected to forms of racist exclusion.

28. Translocally modulating universities are primarily a product of neocolonial franchise arrangements. Financial actors such as NYU and other universities in the USA and Canada are selling their know-how and their personnel to China, India, and the Middle East under the guise of education policy. While not all franchises apply the same working conditions as those prevailing at North American universities, which are guaranteed by labor market legislation and trade-union agreements, the direction in which these translocal enterprises will modulate remains completely open.

4

IN MODULATION MODE
FACTORIES OF KNOWLEDGE

"Welcome to the Machine!" This was the way the university welcomed students in a satiric drawing by the German artist and writer Gerhard Seyfried in the 1970s. Taking a closer look at the drawing, however, the "machine" turns out to be more of a factory, because it arranges the automated mass production of the specific commodity of knowledge in the universities. Seyfried's knowledge factory also has elements of a ghost train (with all kinds of horrifying surprises for those riding it), a flipper device (the students as flipper balls being launched and propelled), a three-tier Nuremberg funnel (knowledge here is funneled in—as it should be in a factory—in masses and anonymized). These kinds of illustrative transfers of central components of the factory as fordist core institution to other institutions have always been widespread. Yet what does it mean, when the metaphor of the factory still continues to be applied to the university, even during the transition to post-fordist modes of production?

Karl Marx developed two different perspectives in the chapter about the factory in *Capital*: from one perspective, it is the "collective laborer, or social body of labor" as "dominant subject" that determines the production process in the "combined co-operation of many orders of workpeople, adult and young, in tending with assiduous skill, a system of productive machines." Here the living labor and virtuosity of the workers is at stake, who are responsible for operating and tending the machines with the help of their skill. Seen from the other perspective, however, the machinery comes into view, "the automaton itself is the subject, and the workmen are merely conscious organs, co-ordinate with the unconscious organs of the automaton, and together with them, subordinated to the central moving-power." Operating the machines here becomes service to the machine, virtuosity is transferred from the worker to the machine, the living labor of the workers is enclosed in the machine. And according to Marx, it is precisely this second aspect that characterizes the *capitalist* use of machinery, the modern factory system.

This view of the factory, reduced to one of two perspectives, as a capitalist usage of machinery turning subjects of production into objects of the machines, and turning machines into subjects, exactly corresponds to Gerhard Seyfried's view of the university as factory: it is not only knowledge itself that becomes a commodity here, but also the knowledge producers' modes of subjectivation—according to Seyfried's picture unambiguously identified as the subordination of the students, who thereafter appear solely as passive components of the knowledge factory, as formatted knowledge *re*producers.

Seyfried's picture, which became well known in 1977 as the cover of the widely read first edition of Wolf Wagner's *Uni-Angst und Uni-Bluff*, identifies the university as factory and machinery: upon passing through the portal, the students immediately find themselves on a conveyor belt. They are sternly and constantly moved along with the aid of various rough mechanisms of drilling and machinic harassment: they are pressed through the gears of basic knowledge, the disciplining sluices of exercises, and the stress-presses of exams, then subject to the imprisonment of administrative rules and the mills of specialized knowledge, until they arrive at the final round of examinations that undertake to include the docile and to exclude the stubborn rejects. Exclusion is drastically imagined here as permanent removal from the knowledge factory, taken to the extreme in Germany of the 1970s as "employment ban" for leftist teachers. Inclusion, on the other hand, means a specific form of the segmentation of space, the hierarchical arrangement in space, literally the imprisonment into space. Within the territory of the university as factory the conveyor belt perpetually conveys the students towards uniformity as standardized graduates.

The main statement of this picture is simple: the university-factory is a monstrous machine, in which initially different and diverse students are turned into uniform people and made fit for exploitation in a uniform society. In light of the advanced conditions of the commodification of knowledge and the striation, homogenization and market-economicization of the universities, of course this metaphor of the university as factory appears more fitting than ever. But it does not go far enough.

Seyfried's picture does not cover the potency of the actors, nor does it cover their entanglements. In analogy to the one-eyed look at Marx's double view of the factory, it emphasizes the students as victims, constructing a sharp opposition between the institutional apparatus and the students dominated by it. It not only misses the contemporary amalgam of repression and students' self-government, but also omits all the other components of the factory university: the teachers in all their hierarchical gradations, the spheres of influence of the administration, and the many aspects of service, from the cleaning crew to the cafeteria and security staff, whether they are tenured or radically outsourced and precarious.

Even the image of the sincere and innocent first-year student, who trips uncorrupted over the threshold of the knowledge factory and is first exposed to the mechanisms of alienation upon entering the institution, is somewhat too simplistic—even for the situation in the 1970s. Today there are more and more experiences and accounts about students, who view their studies from the start purely as a transitional phase between school and job, who regard teaching as a service financed by the tuition they pay, and who accordingly demand their share of co-determination: co-determination no longer as grassroots-democratic self-organization, but rather as a relationship between student-stakeholders and service-providing teachers regulated by exchange value. These kinds of experiences, however, should not be taken as a reason for moralistic pontificating nor for culture-pessimistic ranting about today's youth. Instead, they should be linked with the insight that new subjectivations engender a new necessity to analyze them, and that new critical stances and new forms of resistance emerge from them.

The ideal of a step into the university fostering emancipation from patriarchy, family, school and rural communities presumes that the subjects also want, plan and take this step. Yet the tendency seems to be that the step from the institutions of school and family to the university no longer takes place as a break, but rather as a seamless transition into a mode of existence of growing insecurity. If the transition from the institution of the school into the institution of the university (and perhaps also into the factory) was, in fact, once a promising new beginning, then it is particularly the seamlessness of this transition (like the merging of unpaid traineeships as a student with precarious employment afterward), which indicates that the phases (and their significant territories) previously marked by institutions are becoming indistinguishable, which also indicates the co-existence of various post-institutional forms of precarization. A central component of permanent self-discipline is the concept of life-long learning, but no longer as an emancipatory Enlightenment idea of adult education, as overcoming class boundaries and a vehicle of social ascent, but rather as a life-long (self-) obligation, as an imperative of subservient deterritorialization and life-long prison of continuing education.

The "Postscript on the Societies of Control" is probably Gilles Deleuze's most famous essay. Almost as though in a manifesto, the French philosopher summarizes here the theses of his friend Michel Foucault on confinement (and on its crisis, agony and what follows from that). As marginal as the article may have been for its author, its distribution and reception have conversely had a massive impact. However, the brevity and terseness of the "Postscript" also have a shadow side: despite all its conceptual potential, the weakness of the article lies in the rather un-Deleuzian pattern of a temporal sequence of discipline and control.

What we are experiencing is less to be explained as a linear development from the societies of confinement and closed milieus in the direction of societies of open circulation, but rather as an accumulation of both aspects: also and especially in the context of knowledge production, the social subjugation of worker/student-subjects is compounded by the subjectivation mode of machinic subservience; forced adaptation in the institutional "internment" is accompanied by new modes of self-government in a totally transparent, open environment, and discipline through personal surveillance and punishment couples with the liberal face of control as voluntary self-control.

Modulation is the name of this merging of discipline society and control society: as the aspects of discipline and control are always to be seen as intertwined, their cumulative effect is even more evident in the example of the contemporary knowledge factory. While the students' time is organized in detail in modules, molded, striated, and discipline is taken to an extreme, the modulating state of learning never ends. What Deleuze still described as separated and subsequent attributions for discipline and control flow indistinguishably into one another today: in the new mode of modulation, you never stop beginning, and at the same time, you never finish learning.

The imperative of life-long learning implies a twofold invocation of modulation: an invocation to mold and modularize not only education or work, to stratify, striate and count all relationships, the whole of life, and at the same time an invocation to be prepared to constantly change, adapt, vary. Modulation is determined by this twofold invocation, it is based on the interplay of the clean temporal and spatial separation and striation of the modules with the inseparability of endless variations boundlessly modulating. Whereas modulation means restraint in one case, the insertion of a standard measure, bringing every single module into form, in the other case it requires the ability to glide from one key to another, to translate unknown languages, to interlock all possible planes. If the disposition of modulation consists on the one hand in forming modules, on the other it demands a constant self-(de-)formation, a tendency towards permanent modification of the form, towards transformation, towards formlessness.

In the first section of "Postscript," Deleuze also describes the first four qualities of the factory as an exemplary enclosed environment, the purpose of which is "to concentrate, to distribute in space, to order in time, to compose a productive force within the dimension of space-time whose effect will be greater than the sum of its component forces." It is exactly these reterritorializing qualities of the factory that should be actualized today: concentration, reterritorialization of space and time, composition of a new productive force. In times of machinic subservience and subservient deterritorialization these components of the factory (assembly, occupation and composition) have not simply vanished, but they have to be found today in different forms and places than those that existed during the industrial capitalism of the nineteenth century.

A new generation of activist researchers affiliated with post-Operaism has developed in the last decade, who have taken on current interpretations of the knowledge factory and established their field of action far beyond Italy. Not without reason, in 2006 the transnational network of activists in the field of education gave themselves the name *edu-factory*. The factory that is meant here is again the knowledge factory, but this time in its twofold form: the old figure of the university in its exchange relationship with the purported social and territorial outside, with society and the metropolis, but also the assemblage of institutions and cooperative networks of knowledge production that has become diffuse.

The edu-factory mailing list was started in 2006, dealing with themes relating to the neoliberal transformation of the universities and forms of conflict in knowledge production. What was especially remarkable was the stringency of the instituting process. Instead of installing an open mailing list, the list was initially only opened for two longer rounds of discussion and then closed again—also to the surprise of many list participants. Single authors determined specific thematic lines for one week each with their input. This stringent form imbued the debates with a coherency and intensity that can usually not be maintained for a long period of time on open mailing lists. The first round of discussion focused primarily on conflicts at the universities, the second on the process of the hierarchization of the education market and the potential constitution of autonomous institutions. Specifically these two lines of the relationship of the edu-factory to the university roughly correspond to what was described above as double desertion: desertion here does not mean simply fleeing from the university, but rather the struggle for autonomous free spaces *in* the university and simultaneously self-organization and *auto-formazione* beyond existing institutions.

The example of edu-factory clearly demonstrates the concatenation of social and discursive machines. Just in time for the *onda anomala*, the wave of protests, occupations and strikes at the Italian universities in late 2008, the edu-factory collective published the book *L'università globale: il nuovo mercato del sapere with Manifestolibri*, which was also published in English by Autonomedia in Autumn 2009. The book summarized the most important issues of the online discussions, and in many presentations throughout Italy it has become a catalyst for the discourses fanning the flames of the *onda anomala* and accompanying it. In the introduction to the book there is an interesting contradiction relating to the name of the network, which represents the paradox of the edu-factory. The central slogan is: *Ciò che un tempo era la fabbrica, ora è l'università*. As once was the factory, so now is the university. Yet two pages later, we read that the university does not function like a factory at all. This obvious contradiction will lead us back to the track that the university as factory is no longer to be read only as a metaphor.

Nevertheless, let us return to the association of the university as factory that was established at the beginning of this section, which remains strictly at the level of the metaphor. In the course of the remarkable spread of struggles, occupations and strikes at European universities in recent years, edu-factory organized countless meetings (mostly, but not only in Europe), which primarily addressed the invisible concatenation of these singular struggles. To promote one of these events, which took place in conjunction with the German education strike in June 2009 at the Technische Universität Berlin, the organizers in Berlin used none other than Gerhard Seyfried's picture from 1977, which so strikingly illustrates the university as factory and yet misses the most important characteristics of the transformations of knowledge production in cognitive capitalism. The re-circulation of the simplifying picture and the contradiction in the factory definition of the edu-factory are not based simply on a kind of enchantment with the powerful metaphor of the knowledge factory as an apparatus of repression. Rather, they take recourse—consciously or unconsciously—to the possibility conditions of resistance in the mode of modulation.

If we want to understand today's modes of existence and forms of knowledge production not simply as emerging from the sequence of discipline and control, we must assert a complex and modulating amalgam of social subjugation and machinic subservience, but also draw up possibilities of new modes of subjectivation and forms of resistance, especially taking into consideration the changing complexity of this amalgam. An understanding of modulation as the simultaneity and interaction of discipline and control can neither take recourse to the old forms of resistance in the days of the factory, nor can the resistive counterpart be conceived simply just as a—positively connoted—deterritorialization of control in contrast to—negatively connoted—reterritorializing discipline. The pure invocation of decentrality, deterritorialization and diffusion is not sufficient to draw lines of flight from the assemblage of social subjugation *and* machinic self-government.

The full ambivalence of the knowledge factory in the mode of modulation, its mechanisms of appropriation and its potential for resistance, also allows us to understand the sites of knowledge production not only as sites of the commodification of knowledge and the exploitation of the subjectivity of all the actors, but also and especially as sites of new forms of conflict. And this could ultimately also be the reason for the edu-factory's insistence on a struggle for the traditional site of the knowledge factory, for autonomous free spaces *within* the university. The factory was and is the site of concentration—as far as the valorization of labor and forms of resistance is concerned. In a situation of precarization, but especially of diffusion, of the extreme dispersion of not only cultural and knowledge workers, schools and universities are perhaps the last places where concentration is possible. In this sense, it may indeed be said: What once was the factory, is now the university. And at the same time it is clear that the university assumes new functions as a concentrate in the mode of modulation. Potentially also as a site of immanent desertion, of organizing, of conflict, of struggle.

5

THE SCHOOL OF THE
MISSING TEACHER

Desertion does not mean praise for fleeing from the world, but rather creating worlds. In the context of knowledge production, this power of invention is most likely to be found in self-organized contexts. Nevertheless, there is good reason not to lose sight of the institutional terrain, to use its resources and potentials to try out practices even in the belly of the institution, which are not so easily digestible. For this reason, the starting point here is initially that of an institutional perspective of teaching, not as the opposite of an instituent practice of *autoformazione* and self-organization, yet still as one that is clearly distinguished from it. In the relationship of this strange pair, however, there is sometimes a complementarity, more rarely even a complicity. This complicity between the inside and the outside of an institution goes hand in hand with situative or strategic decisions for overlaps and cooperations, but often enough necessarily also for ruptures and separate paths.

Complicity is extremely fragile, especially as far as the—structurally conditioned—tendency towards co-optation and appropriation by the institution is concerned. A self-critical practice will therefore not strive for a de-differentiation, a blurring of the differences between the inside and the outside of the institution, but rather for temporary overlaps, for precarious processes of exchange and differentiation. In both contexts, in the institution of the university and in self-organized initiatives of knowledge production, and all the more in their overlaps, a common problem inevitably arises: the complex relation between teaching and learning, between differently developed specific competences, between different formal or informal hierarchy positions, between forms of empowerment and of fixing power.

Bert Brecht treated these relations and questions of stance in the interstice between teaching and learning in most of his plays, but especially in those that he called "Lehrstücke" ("learning plays") around 1930. At that time of rising fascism in Europe, the subject matter involved developing an anti-fascist theater practice. Yet this theater did not want to stop at conveying political contents, but instead sought to overturn the hierarchical organizational forms of bourgeois art at the same time. In the tradition of the Russian and German avant-garde of the 1910s and 1920s, the Lehrstück was intended to shift the boundary between actors and audience, to become an "exercise for producers." The lesson of the Lehrstück consisted of playing through all the possible positions and roles, enabling a continual change of perspective. In the first text published under the name Lehrstück, the "Badener Lehrstück vom Einverständnis" ("The Baden-Baden Lesson on Consent"), there is a clear rejection of the conventional relation of instruction between conveying knowledge and drawing lessons as one of a steep transfer of contents. For Brecht, the central effect of theater art as well as for (political) education is the production of a stance: "We cannot help you. | Only a guidance | Only a stance | is what we can give you."

But how can "we" "give a stance"?

The question is certainly not a purely technical one and by no means limited to theater; and it is all the more topical, especially since Brecht's experiments did not lead very far, mired not only in political hostility from the outside, but also in internal contradictions. The question of "giving a stance" problematizes the emergence, transfer and transformation of knowledge; it goes to the foundations of knowledge production and thus—even more pointedly and ambivalently in today's setting of cognitive capitalism—substantially also to the foundations of production as a whole.

The emphasis on the concept of production stands, first of all, for a concrete and clear demand: the relation between teaching and learning is not to be understood as instruction, impartation, nor teachers as the mediators between a static form of knowledge as object on the one hand and those to be taught as subjects on the other. In this paradigm, these kinds of student "subjects" would be considered one-sidedly only in the sense of "subordinates" to instruction, empty vessels waiting to be filled by instructing "imparters." For its part, knowledge filled up in this way would be treated as a fixed parameter, immovable, immutable.

In 1984, in his last lectures entitled *The Courage of Truth*, Michel Foucault distinguished multiple forms of truth discourses from antiquity, of which three can be seen as figures of imparting knowledge: "the prophet," "the wise man," and "the teacher" present themselves as a strongly male-gendered typology, taken from European history. All three modalities of imparting knowledge center around a specific type, who embodies knowledge and represents the center of a hierarchical relationship of impartation.

First the type of "the teacher" as expert. This type involves knowledge that is understood as *techne*, as an ability embodied in a practice. In this mode of embodiment knowledge is owned and passed on from one to another as property, from teacher to pupil in a long chain of tradition, in a hierarchy of generations and a uniform, static order of knowledge. In this order, the various techniques and disciplines are rigidly striated and separated. Against this, instead of reinforcing the bond of filiation and severing the bond of the disciplines, we have to develop a risky practice that seeks conflict and transversal exchange beyond the boundaries of traditions and disciplines.

Secondly, the type of the "wise man": the "wise man" embodies less a technique than a universal knowledge about the being of the world and of the things. His mode of subjectivation consists in fleeing from the world. Since the "wise man" lives withdrawn into himself, his form of imparting can only consist in being a role model, in epitomizing, exemplifying. Yet this form is also a static one, in that his example is understood as being an identitary embodiment, as though it were something constant, only copied in other bodies, adapted to other bodies. Universal knowledge and the status of the universal intellectual as a "wise man" correlates with a disregard for every kind of singularity, specificity, situativity. Yet exactly these three components are to be brought to light in contrast to figures of wisdom.

Finally, the type of "the prophet": "the prophet" also has the role of an imparter, but at the same time, he does not speak for himself, in his own name. Between the present and the future he reveals things that elude human beings. "The prophet" corresponds with the classic figure of the master in art academies. This figure embodies imparting as a medium, as a passageway, as a spiritual center. As enigmatic as the Brechtian message may actually sound, it is impossible to solve the problem of "giving a stance" with a positioning in a prophetic middle between divine truth and the mysterious prophecy of a future fate. Nor is it a matter of speaking in the name of others, representing them or even "helping" them by speaking for them. Nor is it conversely a matter of "assuming a stance," neither in the military sense nor in any other, but rather of moving along a relationship (or multiple posited relationships) without fixing the production of knowledge in a firm center.

A flexible relationship of this kind does not necessarily have to be imagined as a component of the general praise of self-governing flexibility in the paradigm of machinic subservience, but can also describe a specific machinic quality of intellectual exchange. Foucault attempted to distinguish this quality of a critical and flexible relationship in the last years of his life particularly with the Greek concept of parrhesia from the history of antiquity. Parrhesia, truth-speaking, is the fourth form of truth discourse that goes beyond the types of the teacher, the wise man and the prophet. Foucault largely distinguishes three variations for the concept of parrhesian truth-speaking: the political truth-speaking of the citizen to the majority of the assembly or the philosopher to the tyrant, then ethical truth-speaking as Socratic test and exercise leading to care for the self and others, finally the practice of the Cynics as exercising the scandal of the truth, as "philosophical activism" and as a predecessor of the revolutionary movements of the nineteenth and twentieth century.

Even though an actualization of forms of philosophical or intellectual activism may seem substantially more important in times of necessary resistance against neoliberal drilling, what is especially interesting for the question of the relation between teaching and learning is the second, less spectacular variation: ethical truth-speaking, the questioning perfected by Socrates, which leads to self-care. This form of producing knowledge is called ethical, not because it involves the moral integrity of a teacher, wise man or prophet, but rather because an ethical differentiation is at stake as a movement between various positions. These positions (e.g. of teachers and students) are not at all the same, but with Foucault one could say they are in the same boat with all their differentness, in the same situation, sharing specific preconditions.

The focus here is on insinuating a mode of investigation, which leads people to take care of themselves. Socrates is not a teacher in the classical sense, but nor is he a universalist wise man, and nor is he a charismatic master-prophet. His craft consists not of teaching and imparting, but rather in a practice of calling-into-question. The Socratic inquiry leads to self-inquiry. Here knowledge is no longer embodied in a static center, captive, brought to a standstill. Knowledge production lies precisely in the movement from the inquirer to those who are guided by the inquiry to exercise self-care, to give account of the coherence between rational discourse and manner of living.

As an example of the movement from inquiry to self-inquiry Foucault mentions Socrates's procedure for examining the Delphic Oracle, which stated that no one is wiser than Socrates. Socrates himself does not understand Apollo's statement, he does not even attempt to interpret it. Instead, he begins an extensive investigation to test the Oracle's statement. Traveling through the city, he begins an inquiry of the citizens. In a certain way, this procedure treats the same problem that is also central to contemporary techniques of emancipatory knowledge production, essential also for the Operaist practices of *inchiesta operaia* and *conricerca*, or more generally militant research: how is knowledge production to be practiced as a social-machinic exchange, which specifically does not situate knowledge in a privileged center and monopolize it?

"Care for the self" is only to be sought in the movement of the exchange between inquiry and self-inquiry described above, not in the sense of identitary self-positioning, as self-recognition or recognition of the soul, not in the sense of confession and (self-) purging, whether in its Christian guise or its leftist variation (like that of the Maoist self-criticism).

The relationship that focuses on testing the conduct of life and the care for oneself corresponds to a "stance" that is not embodied in an individual; it is instead a paradoxical stance in motion, a moving relation. This kind of relation no longer involves the classical figure of imparting, but rather the movement of the logos, speech itself, or as Foucault wonderfully phrased it in passing in *The Courage of Truth*, a "l'école du maître qui manque," the "school of the missing teacher."

That the teacher is missing, absent, does not mean abandoning every notion of the subject position. It means conceiving subject positionings as machinic relations, positing relations and modes of subjectivation. In terms of the real, the missing teacher, Socrates finds himself in the same position as everyone else, he also has to "go to school." And yet he still has a privileged position that sets him apart from the others: he leads the others to care for oneself and to the potential care for others.

If the teacher is missing, absent, then the middle of knowledge production is no longer the static center of impartation, but rather a rampant middle, not only entraining "the teacher," but also "the wise man" and "the prophet" together with their dual counter-images, the pupils, adepts and disciples. The "school of the missing teacher" can definitely not simply sweep away the relationships of dominance and power in the institutions, the neoliberal forms of governing and self-governing, the problems of privileging and the formation of an elite, the modes of modularizing and modulating knowledge production; however it can negotiate these problems in a new way, surfing on the surfaces of knowledge and at the same time operating in the mode of intensifying, condensing, deepening.

6

INVENTING THE TRANSVERSAL
INTELLECT

There is an odd parallel in the formation of intellectuals in "West and East" in the late phase of the Cold
War. In the dual block system of the 1970s and
1980s there were two specific modes of the subjectivation of intellectuals who dominated the European
scene. In the "East," dissidence resulted in the forced
retreat of thinking into the private sphere. In the
"West" a model arose that also impelled the privatization of the intellect, but in a very different way,
namely as the radical individualization and monopolization of opinion. In the model of the "media
intellectuals," intellectuality was and is little more
than an instrumental function of the mass media.
Intellectuals operate in this function as spectacular
suppliers to the media, supplying a commentary to
any and every topic within the briefest period of time
upon request. Their subject position is characterized
by the narcissist and almost insatiable desire for
media representation. Conversely, liberal media
oriented toward the educated middle class require
the predictable provocations from thundering literati

and moaning philosophers. This form of doubled instrumental media intellectuality is a perversion of the old form of intellectuals that Michel Foucault coined and critically questioned as universal intellectuals. Yet whereas the universal intellectual as advocate and "public man" interpreted the world, if not altogether proposing to save the world, from a site of universality regarded as neutral, the media intellectuals think they *are* the world, and they privatize, popularize and spectacularize thinking.

Beyond both forms of the privatization of thinking, however, new practices of a non-excluding, machinic intellectuality are also emerging, tying into Foucault's figure of the specific intellectual, whose entanglement in local struggles is contrasted with the bird's-eye-view of the universal intellectual. These new practices transgress the privatist model of intellectuality of the solitary thinking, solitary writing and, at the same time, public subject, opening up forms of intellectuality that can be imagined as strictly inclusive and no longer solely available to classic knowledge workers. Intellectuality thus emerging from situativity and sociality speaks for itself, against the background of the specific competence and the concrete situation in which it speaks. It does not have to speak for others, because it comes from the in-between spaces of the general knowledge of society.

Social intellectuality is plural, it is machinic. This is not the vague quality of a "collective intelligence," taking recourse to a communalized pool of know-how, structurally just as identitary and closed as the imagined intelligence of the individual limited by a human body. The betweenness of machinic-social intellectuality and its singular specifics thwart the opposition between individual and collective, relate to the stream of thinking that permeates individuals and collectives, indeed to the possibility of this machinic stream of thinking and speaking itself.

Against the backdrop of the change of modes of production in the direction of cognitive capitalism, in recent years there has been an overlapping of post-structuralist approaches of a critique of representation that goes beyond a speaking in the name of others, and post-Marxist/post-Operaist theorems of mass intellectuality based primarily on the concept of the General Intellect introduced by Marx. In his Machine Fragment, he pointed out that (technical) machines are nothing other than "*organs of the human brain, created by the human hand*; the power of knowledge, objectified." Yet whereas Marx saw this power of knowledge enclosed in the fixed capital of technical machines, machinic intellect today is more living labor than ever. The development of machines, now social machines, which comprise the exchange of technical apparatuses, bodies and sociality, has accelerated tremendously since the nineteenth century, and the "general knowledge of society" has now actually become the "immediate power of productivity."

Post-Operaist theory calls the current form of the General Intellect mass intellectuality: intellectuality of the masses does not at all mean the diffusion of humanist-bourgeois general knowledge into the whole of society, but rather a tendency for the cognitive to become common, at the same time a tendency towards its all-encompassing valorization. The fact that, as Marx writes, "the conditions of the process of social life itself have come under the control of the general intellect," does not have a solely emancipatory quality. The ambivalence of the General Intellect consists in that it has become reality, to a certain extent, in postfordism, yet not simply as control of the many over their working and living conditions, but rather also as a valorization of cooperation and even of thinking. Toni Negri, Paolo Virno, and other post-Operaist writers conceptualized this turn as the "communism of capitalism." The General Intellect and its control over the process of social life degenerate here into an all-encompassing machinic subservience of intellect and language, of information and communication, of imagination and invention.

Inherent to the concept of the General Intellect, even in its emphatic connotation as self-determining the conditions of social life, there are two problems. The first is that the singularities, the specific competencies, the components of an intellect no longer individually embodied, link together in a different way than "generally," if this means the sublation into a universal unity. The second is that the recompositive function of the General Intellect is not to be understood merely as a technical composition or even as a pre-individual precondition of the whole of humanity. Instead, it is the political form of recomposition that must yet be invented. It must be invented and produced, both in production and in political organization. "Knowledge" does not preexist, it is fabricated in exchange. "Organization" does not preexist, it occurs in the concatenation of specific singularities, by no means universally or uniformly.

This is where it becomes necessary to go beyond the General Intellect conceptually as well. The intellect that does not sublate the flows of societal knowledge into a general universal unity, the intellect that is not owing to this kind of unity and does not need to detach itself from it, must be invented as a transversal intellect. This intellect is transversal, because it emerges in traversing the singularities of thinking, speaking, fabricating knowledge: a machinic current of thinking that moves athwart the dichotomy of individual and collective, that permeates the individuals and collectives, populates the spaces between them.

As "organs" of the transversal intellect, the typical intellectual figures of all kinds are in no way suitable, nor are the "organic" intellectuals. Transversal intellectuality is affected by orgic bundles, streams, swarms; nomadic soviets of knowledge production, in a sense, drawing lines of flight from the old models of the avant-garde and universality. These organs are orgic because they unfold in the midst of social machines without simply following or preceding them. Since the beginning of the twenty-first century organs of the transversal intellect have emerged as laboratories of *autoformazione*, which desert the universities and yet still call themselves universities. These are nomadic universities, however: since 2001 the Universidad Nómada in Spain and the Universidade Nômade in Brazil, since 2004 the UniNomade in Italy (since 2010 as UniNomade 2.0), or—with similar concepts, but without reference to the nomadic university—social assemblages like the Free/Slow University in Warsaw, radical education in Ljubljana, keineUni in Vienna, Colectivo Situaciones in Argentina, chto delat in Petersburg and Moscow. In discursive events, art projects, publications and manifestos, these orgic organs join struggles and social movements. They function as instituent machines, when they open up new paths by inventing terms and shifting discourses. They function as abstract machines, repeatedly conjoining knowledge and struggles, as assemblages in the background, sometimes fabricating new micro-machines, sometimes mutating through them, being newly fabricated or modulated by them.

In the breaches of insurrection, rupture, event, the organs of a transversal intellect are neither role model nor vanguard. They permeate everyday life and singular ruptures in a molecular way. They are supportive and cautious, more reticent in the way of Kafka's Josephine: "She does not put it in these words or in any other, she says very little anyhow, she is silent among the chatterers, but it flashes from her eyes, on her closed lips—few among us can keep their lips closed, but she can—it is plainly legible." Teachers, wise men, master-prophets, technocrats, universal intellectuals, prophetic media philosophers, they can all hardly keep their lips closed. The organs of the transversal intellect are the silent abstract machines, and sometimes it flashes from them. The intellect, if it is not avant-garde, not dissidence, not propaganda, not provocation, not narcissism, not spectacle, not advocate, not authorial writer of appeals, not media intellectual newly explaining the world to the people every day, will be transversal, a transversal intellect, emerging in the struggles, in the midst of its orgic organs.

7

"OCCUPY EVERYTHING,
DEMAND NOTHING!"

Three times One of Many: in the fifth week of the
occupation of the Vienna University, in late
November 2009, the Austrian Minister of Science at
the time, Johannes Hahn, initiated a "university
dialogue." Instead of conforming to the expectations
of the ministerial court and properly representing the
occupiers, three actors from the movement were
chauffeured to the "university circus" in a luxury
vehicle. "The Three" wore sunglasses and T-shirts
with the words "One of Many." Neither an act of
representation, nor a nameless and faceless appearance,
it emphasized that the singularities came from the
multitude and would soon happily lose themselves in
the numberless throng of occupiers …

To point out the alibi character of the officious
event—before the "dialogue" the minister had again
called on the occupiers to end the occupation—and
to ironically present their own paradoxical position
in the midst of the logic of representation, they
staged themselves as pop stars. Although they did not
sing, like Kafka's Mouse Folk they celebrated "the

peculiarity […] that here is someone making a cere-
monial performance out of doing the usual thing."
When they spoke about the movement, they were not
speaking for the movement, but from the movement.

The social struggles of recent years form a chain of
reterritorialization, a stream of streaking spaces,
sometimes subterranean, sometimes sweeping everything along on the surfaces of material and media
spaces: free-space movements, struggles to retain
social centers, protests against the limitations of
housing space, university occupations, camps in the
main squares of cities all around the Mediterranean
and beyond. In all of these movements, the occupiers
have shown through their insistence and endurance
that they take the specific spaces seriously in their
materiality and set themselves up to live there, even if
only for a limited time. The occupiers of the central
squares have gone beyond ideas of recoding an empty
middle, and reclaimed an old notion of the public
sphere, the main square as the symbol of democracy.
It is not the symbolism of the evacuated center that
is their focal point of desire, but rather lastingly
streaking the territory, producing a rampant middle
in the tangible and inventive practice of occupation,
exactly there where the territory appears to be completely smoothed, to have dwindled into a plastic
square, apparently unusable for any social practice.

On 15 May 2011 the Puerta del Sol in Madrid
was occupied, shortly thereafter the central squares of
most of the large cities in Spain. With the increasing

displacement of the private and the public sphere these places had also lost the last remainders of their charged function as "public spaces"; now they were smooth spaces, from which every willful determination threatened to slide off. Yet it was exactly these smooth spaces that were appropriated in the occupation. With perseverance and patience, the occupiers developed inclusive practices of assembly in plenums and so-called *comisiones*. While Twitter streams deterritorialized the times and provided cyberspeed turns for the actions and demonstrations, direct communication in the *asambleas* was marked by long, patient, horizontal discussions. And they set up housekeeping, in tents and other transitory domiciles, streaking the clean and smooth territory of the main squares, striating it gently with provisional gardens, info stands, improvised computer networks, soup kitchens and all kinds of other material, and they called it *acampada*, camp. As though to reinforce, stimulate imagination and image production about life in general and in Spain in particular, they seemed to say: yes, our life, life itself, is not clean, not smooth, it is precarious, filthy and fragile.

The reterritorialization of the smooth spaces of the center was followed by a deterritorialization. After several weeks of occupation, the occupiers moved from the centers into the barrios, to decentralize the discussions and actions. Here they began micropolitical struggles against evictions, which they were actually able to prevent in some cases. The real estate bubble drastically exacerbated the housing situation in Spain: not only could many people in search of housing not find any, but because of a credit law, many borrowers had become bankrupt, driven into ruin and out of their homes. The occupiers demanded the right to housing space as a human right and attempted to stop as many evictions as possible. Thus the mutually interwoven movement of re- and deterritorialization did not come to a standstill: on 19 June and 24 July there was another turn towards the center. Taking up the old practice of "star marches," they left the suburbs, moving in July even from the provinces into the capital, again occupying the starting points of their movement.

The movement of reterritorialization that took place in the years prior to this at European universities could be interpreted as being similarly paradoxical as the reappropriation of smooth spaces in the city centers. In Fall 2008, the Italian *onda anomala* set off an endless wave of protests, strikes, blockades and demonstrations that overflowed beyond Italy, to France, Greece and Spain with different emphases. In April 2009, however, something new emerged. The education protests turned into an occupation movement.

The ways in which students and knowledge workers live are marked by dispersion and permanent flexibility. Subservient deterritorialization is their normality. They are perpetually fleeing in all directions, just because they are compelled by precarization to do so. Yet they also produce desires for production in dispersion. Their scurrying back and forth, the streaming, constant overflowing, springing over the boundaries of a tangible and governable community is not only marked by necessity, but also by a desire for fleeing without need. For a multitude so scattered and flexible, however, questions of assembly, condensation, reterritorialization arise, questions of the form and place of reterritorialization. And it has only been a matter of time that the people working in different ways in the university would make their situation in the knowledge factory not only the starting point, but also the focal point of their struggles.

In late April 2009, Zagreb students not only occupied a lecture hall, but even took over the entire Faculty of Humanities and Social Sciences. The department remained under the students' control for thirty-five days, during which the occupation also spread to other cities in Croatia. The complex process of occupation and the detailed regimentation of the entire procedure are well documented in the "occupation cookbook" published by the students in the year following the occupation. The most interesting aspect for subsequent developments was the tendency to a widespread introduction of representation-critical and non-representationist practices. What was already repeatedly foreshadowed in small ways in the social movements of the 1990s and 2000s now began to spread and became a central focus of sociality and organization.

In Zagreb this was initially evident in the constitution of the plenary assemblies. The plenum was principally open, also to people who were not students or employees of the Faculty, and it was the only place where decisions were made. The plenum itself was neither territory nor community, but rather a temporary assembly, which only existed as long as the assembly lasted. Consequently, there were no members, but only the act of assembling, discussing and deciding, without identification and representation.

The other complex of the Zagreb occupation's critique of representation consisted in the media strategy of the occupiers. They purposely evaded the media trap of being identified and instrumentalized as a young, naive and politically somewhat confused protest movement. This image is conventionally introduced as a mainstream media routine, always with the same statements: thoroughly affirmative in the first weeks (It's a good thing for young people to protest!), garnished with "human interest" features of protagonists, only to then turn—also always following the same pattern—into the opposite after a certain period of time. The occupiers are said to be "irresponsible," because they are not represented consistently by the same faces and names, "without a plan," because they present no concrete demands, and finally "prone to violence" in the end.

The Zagreb occupiers undermined this mass media logic by determining their representation strictly by themselves, especially by means of "de-personifying" and the permanent rotation of press speakers, who were principally each only to appear once. The exact articulation of the movement was enabled primarily by the daily authoring of written press declarations. Sending delegates to live broadcasts was rejected multiple times, the representation of the goals of the occupation was kept as far as possible under the control of the collective.

While the Zagreb students were occupying their Faculty, preparations were underway in Europe for larger protests. A one-week education strike was organized in June in Germany, in Italy the wave rose up again to wash over the G-8 Summit of rectors of excellence universities in Torino; at the Vienna Academy of Fine Arts an initially small group of students and assistants organized discussions with members of edu-factory and smaller actions against the approaching introduction of the Bologna reform. In October 2009, four months after the end of the Zagreb occupation, first the Aula of the Vienna Academy of Fine Arts was occupied, then two days later the largest lecture hall in Austria, the Audimax at the Vienna University. This occupation lasted for two months, longer than ever before in Austria.

Under the slogan #unibrennt, there were self-organized lectures, food, living facilities, sleeping arrangements in the occupied university. The territorial expansion first covered the surrounding spaces and lecture halls to establish an infrastructure: soup kitchen, sleeping rooms, queer-feminist spaces, also to protect against sexual assaults, spaces for working groups and additional events. Five days later, the occupation spread to other Austrian cities. By early November there was an incredible chain of Audimax occupations in Germany, Switzerland, in other European countries, but also in California.

From the beginning, the Audimax occupiers operated on the basis of radical inclusion, self-organization and self-administration, declared the plenum as the central location of decisions, and set up a considerable number of working groups. They appointed no press speaker nor any other representatives. They refused to be pinned down to a concrete demand or a fixed catalogue of demands.

With their preconditions of self-administration, critique of representation and insistence on singular voices, the occupiers became extremely conspicuous, atypical assemblages in the dominant setting of representative democracy and spectacular media. Whereas clarity and uniformity of speech, the primacy of the collective and the anonymity of statements were the central achievements in Zagreb, the Audimax occupiers went a step further. The singular quality of the many Ones of Many did not hide behind unity, collectivity and anonymity, but rather conveyed the multitude of positions within the plenum and the differences over forms of organization or ways of dealing with sexist and racist assaults more or less clearly to the outside.

And yet another difference occurred between Spring and Fall 2009, between Zagreb and Vienna:

whereas the Zagreb occupiers only let small portions of the plenum be filmed or photographed, the Viennese took the path of radical publicity. The continual live stream from the Audimax became a cult in the first days of the occupation, not only enabling people outside Vienna to follow the occupation and its self-administration, but also adding further layers to the aspect of direct communication for the local protagonists. Social machines and technical machines interacted; being attached to the electronic gadgets from notebooks to iPhones did not have the character of subservience this time, and the technical procedures of Tweets, live streams and social media created a certain degree of independence from the major mainstream media.

Following the intensive weeks of enthusiasm and with the gradual ebbing away of the streams of bodies and media, a different occupation movement occurred in the terrain of the Audimax, which many regarded as an irresolvable contradiction, as a disintegrating end. With the increasingly cold weather, homeless people mingled with the occupiers. For the Audimax machine of desire, already oscillating between institutionalization and dissolution in its second month, this new turn was too great a task in the midst of the growing difficulties of mobilization. The occupiers gave up before Christmas, the police cleared the Audimax. Yet even though the meeting between the occupiers of the knowledge factory and the homeless assumed a destructive form in this case, resulting in hierarchization and exclusion, just the existential demand for the right to housing space was to lead, as during the sub-prime crisis in the USA or most recently in the occupation movements in Israel and Spain, to a lasting concatenation of the double question of reterritorialization. If reterritorialization is not a movement back to the roots, to identitary origins, which must be repeated again and again, no regaining of homeland or ethnic community, it can take the form of temporary occupation, assembly and condensation, but it also applies to the necessity of an existential break and a new formation of life. The right to housing space is a concrete connector of these two aspects, and groups emerged in Vienna as well, which are much more concerned with this connection since the occupation of the Audimax.

The instituent machine of the Audimax occupation was a factory of the multitude, a gentle streaking, a weak reterritorializing force. The body-machines streaked the Audimax, the traditional center of every-day university life as well as university protests, and fabricated a new territory, overflowing across the walls, through the hallways, into the side rooms, into the surrounding lecture halls. The technical machines, the live streams, Tweets, blogs and clouds, which generated a form of transparency and self-representation through their cloudiness, expanded the following beyond the territory of the university. The social machines experienced self-administration, non-representationist practice and the concatenation of multitude and singularities. No brutal structuring, no conquest of a state apparatus, no massive reorganization of smooth space. A lasting gentle streaking of the territory allowed the practice of the social movement to mutate and become a veritable factory of knowledge in the occupation: "Demand nothing, occupy everything!"

II.

Industries of Creativity

Streaking and Smoothing Time

1

INDUSTRIOUS MICE,
OR STREAKING TIME

To streak time, that means parting time: portioning, dividing up, distributing, a reterritorialization of time. Streaking time means glidingly touching time, creating a space of time in this touch and striating it gently. And it also means that there is another, more complementary than contrary movement: not only streaking as gently striating time, reterritorialization, but also smoothing time, roving in time, deterritorialization.

Among Kafka's "Mouse Folk" there is "scarcely the briefest childhood," no time of carefree roving, but also no time, in which the mouse folk learn to streak their time. From their fertility come ever new and numerous generations, difficult to distinguish in their numbers and in their swarms. From the dispersed multitude of the mouse folk "come pouring at the briefest intervals the innumerable swarms of our children, merrily lisping or chirping so long as they cannot yet pipe, rolling or tumbling along by sheer impetus so long as they cannot yet run, clumsily carrying everything before them by mass weight so long as they cannot yet see." As long as they cannot pipe, cannot run, cannot see, this cheerfully rushing river carries everything before it, endlessly generating a rampant middle, in which things accelerate. But this accelerated cheerfulness does not last long. The children have little time to be children, they cannot be sheltered from the struggle for existence. There is hardly a real time of childhood for the mouse folk, "hardly does a child appear than it is no more a child." With no noticeable transition, the childishly carefree flowing necessarily turns into a hurrying, the river carrying everything before it turns into a permanently driven movement in dispersion. Hurry is the normality of the mouse folk, a restless scurrying back and forth characterizes their existence, subservience to an indistinguishable, incomprehensible goal. The becoming of the mouse folk outruns itself, springs beyond the time, at once becoming timeless, an extreme deterritorialization of time. Whenever and wherever they go, the mouse folk smooth time.

In their hustling and bustling drive, the mouse folk remain childlike, but they also become prematurely old. "We have no youth, we are all at once grown-up, and then we stay grown-up too long, a certain weariness and hopelessness spreading from that leaves a broad trail through our people's nature, tough and strong in hope that it is in general." Forever young, eternally old, the mouse folk move in a blend of heaviness and acceleration. From the modes of subjectivation of an eternal youth of the mouse folk, the relentless bustle, permanent high pressure, and immeasurable hyperactivity arise the weariness and melancholy of hard and long old age. Yet hopelessness is not an existential essence of the being of the mouse folk; it emerges in the times smoothed to the point of timelessness, in which the driven mouse folk age much too soon, have always already been old.

The premature and constant aging also correlates to the purported lack of musicality of the mouse folk, at least as far as singing is concerned: too old, too tired for music, the mouse folk retreat to piping. Supposedly proper music, singing, is left to Josephine, the singer. She is the one who breaks through the timelessness in a rare condensation, "as nowhere else, finding the moment—wait for it—as music scarcely ever does." Josephine creates this moment, she streaks the smooth time of the life of the mouse folk, and she also liberates the mouse folk for a moment. She enters into the dreams of the multitude and sings. Her singing striates the timeless time of the mouse folk, effecting concentration in an otherwise boundless everyday life. "Something of our poor brief childhood is in it, something of lost happiness that can never be found again, but also something of active daily life, of its small gaieties, unaccountable and yet springing up and not to be obliterated."

Josephine's singing allows two different temporalities to cohere: the echo of a miniscule childhood and the present becoming in active life. In the midst of the driven, subserviently deterritorialized life of the mouse folk, a gaiety appears, completely incomprehensible, yet persistent and not to be obliterated. The constellation between the multitude of the mouse folk and the singularity of Josephine is productive, as a trace of gaiety germinates in the melancholy of being tossed around. Yet Josephine's art is also productive in that the hyperactive life of the mouse folk remains subservient, strictly separated from free singing.

The specific relation between Josephine and the mouse folk tends to a one-sided division of time, to a fissure between the constantly roving, eternally young, eternally old mouse folk and Josephine, who seeks to striate her time as an exception. The singer desires an exception from the timelessness of the work of the mouse folk, demanding to be freed from the realm of necessity for her art. Almost already outside the law, art demands exception. But it will not be excepted. "For a long time back, perhaps since the very beginning of her artistic career, Josephine has been fighting for exemption from all daily work on account of her singing; she should be relieved of all responsibility for earning her daily bread and being involved in the general struggle for existence, which—apparently—should be transferred on her behalf to the people as a whole." Josephine's argument for being exempted from the hurried normality of the mouse folk is that conventional work, the exertion and exhaustion that it causes, hinders the greatest achievements in singing. With every means at her disposal, she fights for the highest honor, an unequivocal recognition of her art lasting over time. She argues in different ways, shortens her grace notes, feigns weakness, exhaustion, injuries, hides, and appears to vanish completely in the end.

None of this has any effect. As touched, enthusiastic, adoring as the mouse folk hold to Josephine, so little can they recognize her exemption. They listen to her again and again and reject her demand. No matter what Josephine undertakes, the multitude, the equable mass follows its course undeterred. Josephine cannot be an exception. For the mouse folk, the extraordinariness of her singularity, which consists in her singing, is no reason for privilege. Just as the mouse children cannot be sheltered from the struggle for existence, the artist is not exempted from the hard work of everyday life either.

In "Josephine the Singer, or The Mouse Folk," the deterritorialization of time is initially not to be imagined as anything other than the subservient mouse folk normality of timeless drivenness. The reterritorialization of time, on the other hand, appears in Kafka's story as the demand for an exception that cannot be. Drivenness, subservient deterritorialization on the one hand, striation as production of the exception, privileging reterritorialization on the other. Yet these are not the only possibilities for smoothing and streaking time; the mouse folk also create other worlds.

The subservient deterritorialization, drivenness, timelessness has a flip-side in a different mode of deterritorialization, in the activity, in the bustling drive and liveliness of the mouse folk. Their eternal youth is not only a curse, but also holds the seeds of a reversal, a defection, a fleeing. "A kind of unexpended, ineradicable childishness pervades our people; in direct opposition to what is best in us, our infallible practical common sense, we often behave with the utmost foolishness, with exactly the same foolishness as children, senselessly, wastefully, grandiosely, irresponsibly, and all that often for the sake of some trivial amusement." A quiet laughter also resides in the greatest mouse folk lament. In the midst of the mixture of melancholy and scurrying back and forth, there is also a surplus, in all the subservience there is a desire to not be made subservient, in all the hurried timelessness there is a wild springing out beyond time, an industriousness of the mouse folk.

At the same time, this mode of existence, not only simply losing time, but also surfing on its smooth waves, entails the necessity and the desire to streak the time. The life of the mouse folk is "very uneasy, every day brings surprises, apprehensions, hopes, and terrors, so that it would be impossible for a single individual to bear it all did he not always have by day and night the support of his fellows." It is particularly in the uneasiness and distraction of the life of the mouse folk that the desire is evident for a new form of assembly, concatenation, cooperation without extreme competition. The streaking reappropriation of time should not be imagined as being particulary, as the story of the rejection of Josephine's privilege shows. Yet "the support of fellows" can also not mean referring to forms of solidarity, in which differences are turned into identities and securities are hierarchized. In a world of drivenness and insecurity, a different form of reterritorialization is needed, inclusive and transversal, beyond individual or collective privileges.

There is a turn in Kafka's tale, which almost unnoticeably draws an immanent line of flight out of reterritorialization as exception and towards another refrain: a little mouse, "some silly little thing," is listening enchantedly to Josephine's singing. At the climax of Josephine's presentation, the little mouse begins to absent-mindedly pipe along, disrupts the solemn stillness of the mouse folk, begins its own song. Although for the audience there may be no recognizable difference between Josephine's practiced piping on the stage and the "unself-conscious piping of a child," the little mouse is hissed and whistled down. And yet its utterance is, at the same time, a symptom of the enchantment of Josephine's singing and an act of reterritorialization as self-empowerment, an act of streaking time and space.

The refrain of the little piping mouse is completely different from Josephine's singing. Even though Josephine's performance is itself a weak event, accidental in the everyday life of the mouse folk and their struggles, the piping of the little mouse is unquestionably a much weaker event, accidental to what is accidental. The little mouse's music is perfectly normal piping, not the exception of singing, but rather the diversely practiced singularity of common piping. This also indicates that special privileges can only be where and when every singularity can live out its own specialness, try out its own mode of existence, streak its own time. It is not as an exception, but rather from the multitude that the industrious refrain arises from a little mouse piping nevertheless.

2

SMOOTH TIMES,
STRIATED TIMES

At first glance, it probably seems a bit odd to treat the extension of the factory and ultimately even that of industry with a machine concept in the tradition of Félix Guattari. Whereas in the classical context of industrial capitalism, the terms machine, factory and industry indicate a rising sequence of scale, this quantitative component is not found in a contemporary machinic thinking. Here the concept of the machine goes beyond technical apparatuses to also comprise bodies, things and socialities, their exchange, their movement, and their relations. It does not indicate scale at all. In this sense, there are machines that achieve no material extension whatsoever; their size is thus equal to null. At the same time, there are abstract machines that permeate entire worlds.

In this machinic chaosmos of concepts, it makes little sense to conceive the factory as an assembly of machines and industry as an assembly of factories, in an orderly, linearly rising arrangement. All three levels continue to exist in their old meanings—there are still factories as sheaths for technical machines and the people operating them, there are still various industrial sectors like the coal and steel industry, metal industry, wood industry, weapons industry or pharmaceutical industry. And machines, factories and industries are equally still used as metaphors, for instance when they translate oppressive aspects of mechanized production contexts into the largely immaterial spheres of culture and knowledge production. In addition to this, however, there are striking contemporary meanings that depart from the connotations of the nineteenth and twentieth century. Whereas the machinic in our context applies to composition and movement in all scales, the factory is an indication of condensation, assembly and reterritorialization. It can already be said at this point that industry does not concern the classical understanding as a totality of factories of a certain branch in a certain area, but rather time regimes, the deterritorialization and reterritorialization of time.

In the closed institutions of the industrial disciplinary society, the reterritorialization of time functioned through preceding prior reterritorialization of space. First it was a matter of driving out the "urge to wander" among potential factory workers, coercing them to settle down with the help of new spatial arrangements and introducing new forms of working discipline. The spatially extreme institutions of the factory and workers' quarters already created the perfect conditions for the disciplining and self-disciplining of the worker as a whole. This means that they also had an impact at the time level. Industrial modes of production and existence were conventionally conditioned by a special dictate of time discipline and punctuality: bells, clocks, especially punch clocks, fines for lateness, sometimes even loss of employment for transgressing time discipline. The reterritorialization of workers tending to be nomadic thus functioned not only through the common and rigidly hierarchized spatiality of the factory. It also implied strictly striating and standardizing time.

With their study *Die Fabrikation des zuverlässigen Menschen* (The Fabrication of the Reliable Man), in the late 1970s Heinz Steinert and Hubert Treiber examined in detail the governmentality aspects of the factory discipline of the second half of the nineteenth century and its affinities with the regulations of monastery life. Against the background of "methodical conduct of life (in the sense of constant self-control)," the "propaganda of saving time" became central in the factories of the nineteenth century for adapting people to the rhythm of machines. This also resulted in a new machinic sociality of the workers, in which not only the space of the machines and the spatial arrangement of the factory, but most of all time played a defining role. With the "dictatorship of punctuality" and "bookkeeping of the soul," Treiber and Steinert conceptualized the insight, already gained in the early industrial context, that steering behavior through external compulsion went hand in hand with a willingness to participate voluntarily. Yet it was not only everyday proletarian labor that had to be strictly striated, but the principles of bookkeeping were also transferred to the whole of life conduct. Although the areas of production and reproduction principally remained strictly separated, the techniques of methodical life conduct were applied not only in the factory, but also in the workers' quarters. Not only goods were fabricated, but also modes of subjectivation, of existence and of living. For the "fabrication of the reliable man" it was more necessary than ever to consider conduct not only as repression, but also as instructions for (self-)conduct, as machinic subservience, and to establish the government of time as a central factor of this mode of subjectivation. The reliable man gains the insight that it is better for him to provide his services voluntarily. The reliable man subjects himself not only to the industrial time regime in the factory and the workers' quarters, but also actively participates in its formation and processing. This man doubly serves the machine, modulating all of his time: he serves the machine by operating it, mastering both himself and the machine, but he also serves it by subjecting himself to it.

The striation of time applied not only to working time, but also, even in the nineteenth century, to the total valorization of existence. Here reterritorialization meant taking hold of the entirety of the workers' time; the time regime was not only one of social repression in the striated time of the factory, but also one of machinic subservience, self-discipline and self-control during those times not spent in the factory. For the formerly nomadic workers, this first meant becoming sedentary, then training in community association work, and finally—instead of being purely reduced to a heteronomous cog in a gigantic industrial machine—assuming responsibility for the whole.

Even in the era of industrialization, the total utilization of time already included the phases of the day and of life outside actual working time. And yet these times were at the same time strictly segmented and distinct from one another: the differently striated spaces of the factory and the worker's home marked the strict (gender-specific) differentiation and striation of times.

This concrete form of segmenting time was smoothed with the development of a new paradigm. Modes of subjectivation in dispersion that have developed over the last century are undoubtedly effects of this smoothing process, in which the sites of production become just as diffuse as the times. This does not make the machinic logic of self-disciplining disappear at all; it continues to be in effect under further and further deterritorialized conditions, but also increasingly transgressing the boundaries between production and reproduction, working time and leisure time. Nor does industry disappear, but only shrinks in its familiar form as conjoining territories of disciplining enclosure. At the same time, it proliferates in every possible area of life, even in the formerly strictly anti-industrial areas of culture and creativity.

When Max Horkheimer and Theodor W. Adorno wrote their essay "Culture Industry: Enlightenment as Mass Deception" in the early 1940s as part of the *Dialectic of Enlightenment*, they were objecting to the growing influence of the entertainment industries, the commercialization of art, and the totalizing homogenization of culture, especially in the country of their emigration, the USA. Their skeptical attitude toward the new media of radio and film moved the two authors to cover, in an eloquent style with cultural pessimistic undertones, a broad range of the cultural field with a concept that could hardly appear more alien in cultural spheres: they called production in media and film an "industry." For almost two decades, even after their return to Europe, Horkheimer and Adorno's theses were discussed only among the affiliates of the Institute for Social Research. Over the course of the 1960s, however, their work met with wider reception, finally catching on fully through the updated media critique of the 1970s: the *Dialectic of Enlightenment* became a cornerstone of the literature not only on the ambivalence of the Enlightenment, but especially on the rigorous rejection of an "industrialization" or "economization of culture."

According to Horkheimer and Adorno, the development of the culture industry is to be seen as a delayed transformation of the cultural field catching up with the processes that had led to fordism in agriculture or what is conventionally called industry. Nevertheless, Horkheimer and Adorno regard culture monopolies as weak and dependent in comparison to the most powerful sectors of industry—steel, oil, electricity, and chemicals. Even the last bastions of resistance against fordism finally became factories. The new factories of creativity, newspaper publishing, cinema, radio and television, conformed to the criteria of the fordist factory. The assembly line character consequently structured the culture industry production of creativity in a way similar to agriculture and metal processing before: through serialization, standardization, and the total domination of creativity. In this perspective, mechanization and technical reproducibility lost all the Benjaminian potentials of overcoming bourgeois culture and countering the fascist threat. Contrary to Walter Benjamin's theory of authorship and new media, in which authors could transform themselves into producers by changing the production apparatus, contrary to Bertolt Brecht's "Lehrstück" theory and practice from the early 1930s, in which there are only authors and producers left instead of a consuming audience, Horkheimer and Adorno see only oddly passive producers trapped in the totality of the culture industry. Through the mechanization of art, living labor, now especially its cognitive and creative components, becomes subjugated under dead labor. According to Horkheimer and Adorno, the function of the creativity factories consists not only in the mechanized manufacture of entertainment goods, but also—beyond the conventional areas of production—in determining controlling experience, consumption, reproduction, and it is reproduction that is increasingly adapted to industrial modes of production.

More than half a century later, there is reason to readjust the focus on the function of the culture industry. Instead of regarding the culture industry as something which replaced bourgeois art in the cultural field and transferred a fordist model that was developed elsewhere, outside culture, into the cultural field, the post-Operaist philosopher Paolo Virno asks from the other end of the spectrum about the role that the culture industry assumed with relation to overcoming fordism and taylorism in the second half of the twentieth century. According to his reflections in *Grammar of the Multitude*, the culture industry prefigured the paradigm of post-fordist production. The exemplary character of the procedures of the culture industry then pervaded all other areas. Virno argues that the "archaic incarnation" of the culture industry, investigated in different ways by Horkheimer/Adorno and Benjamin, anticipated the mode of production that later came to prevail in post-fordism generally. Here we thus find a fruitful inversion of the interpretation of the culture industry as a field robbed of its freedom by late industrialization, as conceptualized by Critical Theory: whereas Horkheimer and Adorno call culture industry an obstinate latecomer in the fordist transformation,

Virno sees it as an anticipation and paradigm of post-fordist production.

For Horkheimer and Adorno, the culture industry forms modern culture monopolies, but also at the same time the economic area in which some part of the sphere of liberal circulation is allowed to survive, along with the corresponding entrepreneurial types, despite the process of disintegration elsewhere. Although some small spaces of difference and resistance still emerge within the totality of the culture industry, difference must secure its survival by becoming assimilated in this totality.

In this description, difference serving to achieve new levels of productivity is nothing but a vestige of the past, which is cast off in the general fordization of the culture industry as a remnant. From Virno's perspective, these purported remnants can be regarded as premonition, omen, anticipation. The culture industry proves to be not merely a weak and late-coming industry in the process of fordization, but also a future model and anticipation of the wide-spread post-fordist production modes: informal, non-programmed spaces, open to the unforeseen, communicative improvisations that are less a remnant than a core, less margin than center. This applies not only to new forms of culture industry, but also to the entirety of social production, including the "old" forms of industry.

The institutional form, in which the culture industry developed in the mid-twentieth century, is that of the gigantic music, entertainment or media corporations. According to Horkheimer and Adorno, creatives find themselves administered and enclosed as employees within an institutional assemblage, in which their creativity is repressed through the form of dependent labor. In *Dialectic of Enlightenment* this connection between creativity-constraining employment and social subjugation is generally described as the "self-derision of man," specifically of the "liberal man," who thus loses any possibility of becoming an entrepreneur.

Just as hopeless dependency and social control generally predominate in the world of employees, even the last resort of autonomy, the production of creativity (and here there is an early echo of the romanticism of artistic autonomy in Adorno's later work, *Aesthetic Theory*), is described as striated, structured and stratified, and the majority of its actors originally regarded as resistive are finally civilized as employees. In return for the employees letting themselves be tamed, the institution promises a certain degree of control over irresolvable contradictions and social security for the employees. Even if the specific institutions of the culture industry do not last forever, their apparatuses are intended to create this impression specifically because of their apparatus nature and to exonerate the subjects in this way.

Even if we accept this one-sided structural view for early forms of the culture industry, it seems that something changed here at the end of the twentieth century. The assemblages that are today labeled as creative industries are no longer structured in the form of huge media corporations, but mainly as micro-enterprises of self-employed cultural entrepreneurs in the fields of new media, fashion, graphics, design, pop, etc., conceptualized at best in clusters of these micro-enterprises. So if we ask about the institutions of the creative industries, it seems more appropriate to speak of *non*-institutions or *pseudo*-institutions. Whereas the model institutions of culture industry were huge, long-term corporations, the pseudo-institutions of creative industries prove to be temporary, ephemeral, project based. The time of the modulating project institution is perfectly smoothed, but by no means eternal. At the same time it is striated, modularized, and multiply hierarchized in a new way.

These project-based institutions seem to have the advantage of being grounded in self-determination rejecting the rigid order of fordist regimes. Instead of the old institutional task of exonerating and managing contradictions, however, they conversely promote precarization and insecurity. In fact, it is clear that a glaring contradiction is evident in the idea of "project institutions" in relation to their temporality: on the one hand there is the long-term exoneration that the concept of the institution implies, and on the other, the project is specifically based on the premise of a distinct time-limit.

Whereas Horkheimer and Adorno still deplored the fact that the subjects of culture industry as employees lost their opportunities to become freelance entrepreneurs, it seems that in the present situation this problem has been completely reversed. The freelance entrepreneur has become a hegemonic pattern. And even the successors of the twentieth century culture industry, the major media corporations, conduct a policy of outsourcing and contracting sub-companies under the banner of entrepreneurship. In these newer media corporations with their convergence from the field of print to audiovisual media all the way to social media, all that remains for permanently employed workers in many cases—and this applies even to public service media—are only a few core management functions. In contrast, most of the people labeled as creatives, work part-time, freelance and/or as self-employed entrepreneurs with or without limited contracts. Somewhat cynically one could say that Horkheimer and Adorno's complaint about the loss of entrepreneurial freedom under post-fordist working conditions has now been perversely redressed: the creatives are released into a specific sphere of freedom, of independence and self-government. Here creativity becomes the imperative, flexibility becomes a despotic norm, the precarization of work becomes the rule. Time can no longer be clearly assigned according to dual parameters like work and leisure, production and reproduction, employment and unemployment, but is striated and smoothed beyond these designations. At the same time, the whole of time is fragmented and hierarchized in many different temporalities that cause all earlier forms of striating time to become frayed: for instance, a time of a poorly paid or unpaid internship, a time of looking for work with or without pressure from the employment office, a time of preparing new projects, a time for unpaid practices of self-organization, a time for paperwork, a time for electronic correspondence, a time for brief regeneration, a time of training and continuing education, a time for socializing—whether in direct communication or through social media, a time for developing networks, a time for unpaid sick leave, a time for dealing with bureaucracy, and sometimes several of these at once.

The increasing smoothing of fordist dual temporality goes hand in hand with a multiply divided and hierarchized process of striating time. Describing this process with the economicization of culture or the industrialization of creativity is insufficient. In fact, this involves a spreading modulation of creativity, a modulating and modularizing valorization of the times of creativity. This modulation bores deep into the interstices of individuals and collectives, into their modes of subjectivation and forms of living, and it contributes to the rise of new machinic subserviences, but perhaps also ultimately to a dead end for this specific form of valorization. Whereas access, as total as possible, to the entirety of time and its many territories seems to be a veritably endless source of new possibilities for commodification, this access—if we think the total valorization of living labor all the way through—also has the potential to consequently exhaust this source. Present becoming is the time of creativity, and should the time come that we never arrive in this extended form of the present again, then it can happen that simply nothing more happens, nothing more occurs, nothing more is created than a difference-less repetition of the eternal same.

3

SEVENTEEN TENDENCIES OF
THE MODULATION OF CREATIVITY

We are cogs in an increasingly modularized society, and at the same time we modulate ourselves and the world. This double modulation means a constant reforming and deforming of our times and an ever more detailed grip on its modules. Invocations of creativity aim at the deforming smoothing and the scoring striation of times, at a grip as extensive as possible on our not yet commodified resources. Far beyond the discourse of the economicization and industrialization of creativity in the conventional sense, it is now no longer a matter of the becoming-commodity of culture, but rather of economies of desire, of a subservient modulating of our desires and their disciplining modularization.

1. The "independent artist" serves as a model for the modulation of cultural work in the direction of celebrating entrepreneurship, self-entrepreneurship and founder myths. What was once projected onto independent artists as the autonomy of art, is now expected of a field of cultural work that is fraying and unraveling more and more.

2. The privilege of "independent art" has always been a myth, but invoking it today becomes more grotesque than ever. Together with the praise of an independent, entrepreneurial artist life for as many as possible, a system of measuring and striating is introduced in all areas of art production, also in the narrower sense: from artist ranking to the academic striation of PhDs for artistic research all the way to the index numbers of art institutions as central legitimation for public funding.

3. Despite comparably higher qualifications, art and cultural workers have to accept below-average incomes. Attempting to link this imbalance to the relatively high participation of women in cultural work and denouncing it as a "feminization of cultural work" is a discursive reversal of economic inequality.

4. Whereas salary rates and fee guidelines exist for employees and freelancers in other branches, wage dumping predominates in cultural work not only for interns, ranging all the way to the frequent suggestions from commissioners, whether benevolently naive or purposely exploitative, that the freedom of art means artists should work for them for free.

5. The institutional form of this (self-) exploitation is the paradoxical establishment of the project institution. It is institution to the extent that it foregrounds responsibility for the self-entrepreneurs in cultural

work, project to the extent that it immanently aims at completely taking into service the time of the participants and simultaneously stresses the time limit of the enterprise.

6. Not only in the new pseudo- and project-institutional organizational forms of the cultural self-enterprise, but also in the large cultural and media institutions, a practice is developing of outsourcing all functions that do not concern internal management. The so-called creatives are especially affected by this.

7. The generally propagated "culture of self-employment" and the concrete forms of the self-enterprise and the project institution create insecurity, also for all of those who previously provided services in cultural work in various contract forms of their own volition, or alternated between employment and entrepreneurial work.

8. The various forms of dependency in self-employment are subject to different legal regulations in almost every single case, often bundled in their diversity in single individuals. The areas of contracts and taxation thus become an impe-netrable legal jungle, creating new dependencies.

9. The freedom and independence of "independent contractors" and the "new self-employed" has the effect of outlawing them not only in an economic

sense. The permanent situation of insecurity, risk and precarization results in new illnesses. Stress, depression, nervous disorders and other psychopathologies characterize precarious everyday life.

10. Insurance systems hardly react to these new economic, legal, mental and physical conditions of precarity. On the contrary, with growing complexity, by constantly raising rates and reducing benefits, they tend to exacerbate insecurity.

11. The immaterial modes of production in cultural work produce all possible surpluses in the form of commodifiable rights. In the fight over image rights, right of publicity and copyright in general, no matter how much cultural producers take a stand for Creative Commons and against the monopolization of immaterial rights, they are increasingly disenfranchised and dispossessed, used at best by corporations as symbolic shields for their business interests.

12. Where art institutions regard themselves as critical, they are increasingly losing state support. In many cases, this leads to the surrender of significant positions, to self-censorship and to intensified conflicts between the institution and critical art producers. New, old institutional figures emerge at the same time. In their programs, market-compliant and conformist strategies are coupled with hollow

spectacular peaks, and outsourcing and precarization predominate in their apparatuses.

13. The discursive enforcement of the modulation of creativity permeates all social fields and the most diverse geographies. It is accompanied by campaigns based on hollow propaganda terms like creative entrepreneurs, creative clusters, creative districts, creative cities. As they penetrate into cultural policy programs, their process of hollowing out is brought to culmination: cultural policies abolish themselves.

14. Together with the celebration of creative industries as a rising economic profit zone, on the drawing board of creative consultants there is a grotesque expansion of the area of creative industries, which is now to encompass viniculture as well as software, organization consultancy and carpentry. With the help of empirical studies and "creative industry reports," agencies and state administrations construct an economic zone trumpeted as the second or third largest "industry" in the major European countries.

15. Creativity is increasingly also conquering a fixed place in the portfolios of urban planning. For locational advantages on a global level, for the "upgrading" of entire cities under the title "creative city," for the gentrification of city districts into "young creative districts," cultural capital is an obligatory program.

16. Whereas multicultural aspects play an important role in the future scenarios of the planners, racist exclusions striate the creative scenes at the same time. Migrants are usually among the first objects of gentrification that have to give way to these creative scenes. Visa regulations and residency permits are conventional means of exclusion in the cultural field as well.

17. Creative consultants and planners compose the opera in which they want to play the main role. First a clever, superficial book that is made into a bestseller, then every month another incredibly well paid performance for the mayor of yet another metropolis, and in the end a modulating life in the beautiful creative city, where privacy means gated community and public means a perfectly smooth space.

4

THE INDUSTRIAL TURN

Cultural industries, the creative class, creative industries. It seems as though the old, rigid discourse of industrialization from the nineteenth century has taken over the smooth spaces of immaterial, cognitive and creative labor at the turn of the twenty-first century. What can it mean, when the apparently so different and contrary terms of creativity and industry conjoin? And what does this conjunction mean, especially when the two areas can no longer simply be separated from one another? In formulations like *creative industries* or *cultural industries* there is clearly more at stake, namely a blurring, a merging, an overlapping of spaces that used to be cleanly segmented and separated: the becoming-industry of creativity and the becoming-creative of industry.

In the art field, where myths of genius, originality and autonomy are still more virulent than ever, despite countless funeral orations, these topoi of the "economicization" and the "industrialization" of culture are almost eternally repudiated, contrary to clear evidence of the art market. Even today, sixty years after the late publication of the *Dialectic of Enlightenment*, industry is still not much more than a pejorative epithet in the sublime fields of art.

So it is all the more a question of how it could happen that with a simple shift from singular to plural, from *culture industry* to *creative* and *cultural industries*, specifically this brand term has today been reinterpreted as a kind of universal promise of salvation—not only for a few politicians, but even for many actors in this field themselves.

There are three complementary interpretations that explain the strange conceptual paradox of the "creative industries": the first interpretation seeks to outline the cultural policy backgrounds, the second looks more closely at the divisions and differentiating hierarchizations of the field that can be explained sociologically, and finally the third examines its dominant modes of subjectivation.

The first interpretation that suggests itself is that in the early 2000s, as the term *creative industries* became successively established throughout Europe in cultural policy programs, state funding for art has been increasingly redistributed from programs that presented critical positions to uncritical positions or commercial enterprises. Of course, critique has always been marginal and resistance has always been found co-opted in one or the other way, but in a strange meeting of educated middle class affirmation of critical stances and the euphoria of 1968 in relation to emancipatory effects of cultural work, sub-cultural and counter-cultural spaces were subsidized again and again in the 1980s and 1990s. Despite being state funded, these spaces developed specific practices of immunizing themselves against becoming instrumentalized by the state apparatuses, but now their existence is threatened. In addition, there is an endeavor to severely push back state funding for culture, which is highly developed in the European welfare states, in conjunction with neoliberal and national-populist transformations, or at least to manage this funding more and more according to economic aspects. This development functions as part of a European-wide process of shifts in cultural policy, which—starting with Tony Blair's politics in the 1990s—is intended to "de-politicize" state-funded art production: to do away with the remainders of cultural production as dissent, as controversy, and as the creation of public spheres; to promote creative industries as a pure and affirmative function of economy and state apparatus. This also explains the shift in terminology in cultural policy programs from emancipatory and social-critical elements in the direction of issues of social integration and the creative industry. The fog machines of creativity—"creative economy," the "creative class," "cultural entrepreneurs," and the "creative industries"—have been influential propaganda tools in this process.

However, it is not only the populist-neoliberal strategies of today's politics that are relevant to the genealogy of this development, but also certain programmatic guidelines of social-democratic cultural policies in Europe after 1968. Emancipatory social-democratic programs of the 1970s, which actually go back to revolutionary concepts from the 1920s, propagated slogans like "culture for all" and "culture from all." These large-scale starting points for a "democratization of culture" were not only intended to enable workers to access the bourgeois consumption of culture, but also to counter the "idolatry of sublime art" with a "secularized" cultural production—this was at least the goal of several generations of socialist and social-democratic cultural policies of the twentieth century. Today, their concepts surprisingly seem to be increasingly realized, but in a completely inverse form. "Culture for all" implies the culture-political obligation of art institutions to push quantity and marketing in a populist spectacular way, and in its perverted form, "culture from all" indicates an all-encompassing (self-) obligation to be creative. State apparatuses no longer need repression here to appropriate creativity and participation, sociality and communication. On the one hand they insist on striating and measuring mass consumption of culture, and on the other they retreat to a modulating invocation of creativity and cooperation, activation and subservience of the desiring machines.

However, the paradox of the term creative industry can also be explained with the tensions, divisions and re-orientation of various parts of the cultural field. The leading terms of creative industries discourses, which superficially appear synonymous, such as "digital boheme" and "creative class," refer to quite different and discriminable partial fields. Behind the terminological division into techno-trendsetters immanent to the art field on the one hand and a fraying "class" of cultural work as modulating creativity on the other, there is perhaps even the old phantasm of the avant-garde pressing on ahead and the masses obediently running along behind.

The narrower field of art production is always developing new techniques and media, but it is still sharply separated from the industrial paradigm. As much as artistic practice itself works against the modus of originality and has played, at the latest since Warhol, with industrial manufacture, the rules of the art field and especially of the art market still circle just as resistantly around the distinction potentials of an anti-industrial imperative. Even in their negation, creativity and originality remain necessary resources of capital, often hidden, yet at the same time too easily recognizable in the opposition of the artist habitus to every form of industry.

In contrast, a broader field of cultural work relies on climbing the social ladder and penetrates into the cool new field of creativity, or at least what is imagined as such. Here the industries of creativity, with their flair for obstinate self-design, produce an aura that at least appears more positive than other areas of services. Belonging to an imaginary "creative class" promises a better life as creative directors, web designers and fashion people. The precipitous transition from self-exploitation as a cultural entrepreneur to extreme precarization is quickly completed, however. At the low end of the scale, then there is still the pat on the back from cultural policies for all the creative people in voluntary work and for some the affirmative exploitation of creative exhibitionists in casting shows and reality soaps.

Whereas the narrow art field and the wide "class" of potential creatives, in other words both components of a blurred concept of creative industries, can be quite easily distinguished from one another in their differential hierarchization from the sociological perspective, the term industry, on the other hand, leads to a congruent and almost unbounded meaning for both components: as a description of a particular time regime, which adds an aspect of subservient deterritorialization to the reterritorialization of time in the era of industrialization.

A third explanation for the conceptual paradox of creative industries arises from a closer look at the modes of subjectivation in the fields, structures and institutions that were and are described with the terms culture industry and creative industries.

First of all, a look at the terminological difference suggests itself here, which makes up the difference between the branding of culture industry and creative industries: whereas culture industry still seemed to emphasize the structural and abstractly collective components of culture, an implicit invocation of the productivity of the individual occurs in the creative industries. This kind of difference between the collective and the individual only exists, however, at the level of invocation; the becoming-industry of creativity is characterized specifically by being athwart to this dualism.

In the interpretation of the Institute for Social Research, the unified form of culture industry is, first of all, the institutional structure for modes of subjectivation that subjugate the individual under the power and the totality of capital. The function of culture industry is that it encloses, counts and striates its audience's body and soul. At the same time, it exposes this enclosed audience to a permanently repeated, yet ever unfulfilled promise, generating a desire and continually suspending this desire in an unproductive way. This is what makes the core of the idea of culture industry an instrument of mass deception: the culture industry deceives, makes compliant, subordinates. And at the same time, moments of self-deceit, casual obedience, subservience are also components of subjectivation in the network of the culture industry.

Even in the seemingly so structural, homogenizing perspective of Horkheimer and Adorno, modes of subjectivation and desire production thus also play a role. Desire and enslavement coincide, as in the famous passage from *Dialectic of Enlightenment*: "As naturally as the ruled always took the morality imposed upon them more seriously than did the rulers themselves, the deceived masses are today captivated by the myth of success even more than the successful are. They have their desires. Immovably, they insist on the very ideology which enslaves them." As in other formulations in the *Dialectic of Enlightenment*, an ambivalence is suggested here, which if it does not quite conjoin self-active subservience and externally determined subjugation through a totalizing system, at least places them next to one another on an equal level. Subservience and subjugation are simultaneously existing poles that are actualized in the same things and in the same events. In the mode of social subjugation, a higher entity constitutes the human being as subject, which refers to an object that has become external. In the mode of machinic subservience, human beings are not unified subjects, but are, like tools or animals, parts of a machine that overcodes their concatenation. The interplay of the two regimes is particularly evident in the phenomenon of the creative industries, two parts that perpetually reinforce one another, whereby the components of machinic subservience grow in significance due to a surplus of subjectivation. *Asservissement machinique* is what Deleuze and Guattari call the relevant concept, and this subservience is accompanied by service, servility and obedience. "Should we then speak of a voluntary servitude?" is the rhetorical question in *A Thousand Plateaus*, and the answer is no: "There is a machinic subservience, about which it could be said that it appears as reaccomplished; this machinic sub-servience is no more 'voluntary' than it is 'forced'."

Machinic subservience, and in it the centrality of desiring production and servility, is exemplified in the gray area between consumption and production. For Horkheimer and Adorno, already in the 1940s, the actors in radio talent competitions being "denied any freedom" in the 1940s were functions of the business. Controlled and absorbed by talent scouts, talented performers belong to the industry "long before it displays them; otherwise they would not be so eager to fit in." In light of its updated version in Reality TV, docu-soaps and casting shows, in fact the image of extras that appear to be protagonists seems more plausible today than ever. Looking at a broader idea of producers producing and presenting not only materialized cultural goods, but also affects and communication, we see the picture of an activating system determining every move and every mood growing even darker.

The mere appeal is sufficient: Be creative!—and the creative sheep are happy, as long as sheer pressure, anxiety and existential worries do not render them incapable of creativity. Everyone is an artist, so he or she should also work and live in a way that is accordingly flexible, spontaneous and mobile, or self-exploiting, without security and forced into mobility.

The minor shift from culture industry to creative and cultural industries and their discursive success story are largely due to the way that the modes of subjectivation of machinic subservience are associated with desire as well as conformity. Desire and servility are the central components of machinic subservience. It is only with the help of the economy of desire that time can be subserviently deterritorialized and reterritorialized.

Yet these same fields of the economy of desire also open up escape routes from subservience. There are desiring machines that compose into a different industry, concatenate into a different industry, produce an industry different from the entrepreneurial start-ups of the creative industries, and this other industry has not always been servile.

Industry has not always been what it became in the course of the nineteenth century. *Industria* is a Latin word that meant roughly "activity," "diligence," "industriousness." Composed from the components "indu-" and "struo," it referred to an activity of "building," of "setting up," which took place "inside," a process of making within domestic economy. This line of meaning introduced through French was still widespread in German in the eighteenth century. Industry designated a personal trait, disposition, virtue, and at the same time it also held an economic aspect that soon went far beyond housekeeping: invention and assiduity are the central components of this old concept of industry.

Starting from this arrangement of personal dispositions revolving around invention and assiduity, collective notions of industry developed in modernity, especially as a policing appeal to the population to greater industriousness and thrift. In the late eighteenth century, "culture of industry," "increase of industry" meant primarily steering the inventive industriousness of the individual in the direction of increasing national productivity. In Germany, "industry schools" and an entire "industry-pedagogical" movement even developed against this background. Their task was, not least of all, the administration of the economy of time, instructions for the efficient use of time, and here there was already evidence of the exploitability of time as a whole (beyond working time in the narrower sense). The industrial invention was made servile for the purposes of a time-saving economy also taking all "accidental times" into service.

In French, on the other hand, *industrie* was understood since the end of the Middle Ages as the ability to do things differently, to use the intellect for new paths. Here, industry as "inventive industriousness" is more than only mechanical assiduity in the service of the national economy. It is inventive ability and, at the same time, assiduity, persistence, drive. There is a component of industry that exceeds the economic circles of time efficiency, which does not make ingenuity and industriousness servile, or at least not to such an extent. This meaning still seems to be preserved today in the English word *industrious*. This is also the meaning that can be actualized for a mode of subjectivation that reappropriates time: *industria* as an inventive reappropriation of time, as a wild and no longer servile industriousness allowing smooth and striated times to newly emerge in the flows of reterritorialization and deterritorialization. An industry that is no longer creative economy, but rather *busyness* in the vernacular, a wild, disobedient, orgic industry.

This in turn also reveals the full ambivalence in the title of this chapter: "industrial turn" is by no means to be understood in the sense of the many "turns" invoked in social sciences, cultural studies or literature studies, which seek to name a (social) transformation that has already taken place and describe it as clearly as possible. The term "industrial turn" is not intended to simply empirically cover the transformations leading from classical industry through the culture industry to the industries of creativity. It is intended to make the term industry itself iridescent, to newly invent the other industry that breaks through conventional time regimes. So "industrial turn" does not imply a descriptive procedure, but rather a desideratum that is just emerging, although its genealogical lines can be traced far back into the industry history of the cultural field.

5

ISLAND INDUSTRY

In the late nineteenth and first half of the twentieth century, Isola was mainly a meso-industrial territory at the edge of Milan. The former agrarian region before the gates of the city—in the area of the so-called Corpi Santi—had been increasingly industrialized in the 1880s and 1890s. Over the course of time, large factories that were further and further extended produced electro-technical machines and equipment for the international corporation Brown Boveri. Part of this factory, the "Stecca," built in 1908, was later sold to Siemens. In addition, there was a comb factory, a soap factory, a larger forge and several smaller facilities; finally, there was the railway warehouse behind the extended tracks laid to transport goods in and out, which together with two canals separated Isola from the rest of the city and gave it its name ("Island"). On the whole, the expansion of the factories in the first decades of the twentieth century resulted in the emergence of a small city within a city.

The industry undoubtedly implied a hard life for the workers: the hard work in the plant, the gender-specific striation between production and reproduction, the lack of social insurance, especially at the beginning of industrial capitalism. And yet the workers lived in a social environment that also allowed them a certain sociality and the development of specific modes of subjectivation. The industry required not only workers, but also craftspeople to supply parts. Workshops were thus established in the inner courtyards of the residential blocks, which are partly still in use today. Isola became a mixed worker and crafts quarter. The factories were often surrounded by workers' housing estates, such as in Lunetta, a half-moon-shaped area in the south of Isola, an arrangement that enabled social intercourse during working time as well as leisure time. Party and union ensured a clear order in politics. And when conditions of exploitation went too far, there were also well tested forms of resistance and struggle, from sabotage to strike. Not least of all, the island situation also provided shelter for communists, petty criminals and partisans on the run.

Various factors in the second half of the twentieth century led to a process of de-industrialization, which resulted in the 1970s in the dereliction of large industrial complexes throughout Europe in the inner areas of metropolises and larger cities. What happened with the partially gigantic architectures? A relatively widespread phenomenon was that of squatting, the reappropriation of the industrial spaces by counter-cultural initiatives, which no longer turned their attention (only) to large, molar politics after 1968, but rather to everyday practices and molecularity. For these molecular experiments, the old industrial complexes were welcome sites for trying out alternative modes of living and production.

Industrial ruins in central or particularly exposed situations that were in danger of becoming objects of speculation, were saved from demolition by squatters in several places in Europe—and some of them were even placed under protection as historical monuments later. Squats emerged in a spectrum of interim use by artists all the way to long-term socio-cultural occupations (also as predecessors of the radical autonomous occupation movement in the 1980s). The difference of these various artistic, social and socio-cultural uses also had significant effects on the sustainability of the occupations for the respective quarters.

To some extent, Isola and its vacant factories were predestined for this kind of mixed career of appropriation: close to the city center, diverse post-industrial architectonic infrastructure, but most of all an intact and mixed social structure of residents were crucial factors as well. In the social mix of those involved in the reappropriation of the island industry, again and again there was also a considerable portion of art producers. Strangely enough, however, the artists who should have had a certain training in social contextualization against the background of the practices of institutional critique in the 1970s and of context art in the 1980s were largely missing from involvement in transversal activist practices. In 1973, the US American artist Gordon Matta-Clark, known for his anarchitectural and site-specific works, used the abandoned electrical engineering factory Brown Boveri for the early *cutting* (as Matta-Clark called his building incisions) with the title *Infraform*. Two years later, he made a clearer decision for a politically connoted art practice in the context of *lotta continua* in a different occupied factory in Milan. In the narratives of the artistic utilization of Brown Boveri from Fall 1984 to Spring 1985, on the other hand, there is a plethora of romanticizations of industrial architecture. The perspective of the artists remained fixed on the overwhelming dimensions of the spatiality; it was obviously the attractive aesthetics of the ruins that primarily induced them to carry out their works in an industrial production space. Without wishing to denounce individual actors—the point here is the differentiation and critique of the discourse predominant at the time—the artistic function of the post-industrial ruins consisted primarily in their use as spectacular scenery for installations and other artistic works.

This function of post-industrial aesthetics and the interior and exterior space of the factories implies multiple partial aspects: first of all, there is an idealization of the late victory of nature over industrial civilization. The agrarian spirit of the Corpi Santi returns, so to speak, and celebrates its post-industrial resurrection. Cats and rats that inhabit the factory halls, overgrown brush and weeds proliferating over the technical equipment, these are all familiar metaphors for the reversal of the alleged domination of technology over nature. A ghostly reprise of the luddite humanism of the nineteenth century inheres to these metaphors, and the reprise of the false dichotomy of technology and nature, of man and machine. Yet whereas the luddites of the nineteenth century still had their sights set on capitalist exploitation, despite their abbreviated humanist ideology, the aesthetic-architectural perspective of the Brown Boveri artists in the late twentieth century were not interested in these kinds of social issues. For the artists, the factory ruins were not only a symbol of an anachronistic "back to nature," but in their monumentality they were also a kind of church substitute. They called the largest hall of Brown Boveri "Cathedral," alongside which there were works referring to "altar" and "sacristy." Finally, as the climax of this sacralization, the romanticism of "the last time" became evident in the desire to animate the doomed industrial architecture one last time before the spectacular act of demolition. In a *Flash Art* article in 1985, for instance, Giulio Ciavoliello wrote about the "dream" of the artists in Brown Boveri: "… il sogno, durata dall'autunno alla primavera, di rianimare per un'ultima volta questo edificio."

The socio-cultural centers of the 1970s represent a stark contrast to the romantics of ruins and the celebration of impending demolition. Their functional interest focused less on the looming end of the pseudo-sacral architecture than on using the post-industrial structures as long as possible. Instead of the single-issue background of the artists, there was a transversal quality to be found in the social composition of the socio-cultural centers. This comprised social initiatives, crafts, workshops, ateliers, rehearsal spaces and concert halls with the charm of permanent breakdown (the exchange between artistic practice and architecture was most intensively cultivated in *Industrial* and early techno practices). At that time, artists were also naturally often part of the movements, sometimes with complete integration taken for granted, sometimes more ephemerally as a critical margin.

The smaller and larger industrial quarters at the edges of European city centers were initially spared from the grip of speculation. Since the late 1990s, however, in conjunction with the extension of urban expansion processes, there have been massive urban planning attacks on these areas. These takeovers often do not fit in the pattern of gentrification, because they only partially relate to residential areas, and when they do, these are the residential areas of population segments that have little or no political representation, in other words no influence whatsoever on decisions about their territory. In those areas, mainly large-scale post-industrial ruins far away from the center, high gloss brochures are often not even needed to take on the revalorization of the territory. This is different in urban areas, in which long-standing existent social infrastructure collides with a post-industrial after-use. Here a complex process of exercising domination between social subjugation and machinic subservience is required. Today Isola appears to be an exemplary case of this kind of soft gentrification. A mixed population, a large proletarian and migrant portion, hardly any larger thorough-fares, small public parks where residents meet, these are ingredients that do not simplify a takeover by real estate corporations—and which enhance their desire immeasurably at the same time.

So it is in Isola as well. During the 1980s and 1990s the quarter was hardly disturbed by urban planning intervention endeavors. The Stecca, the bar-shaped former Siemens factory, was taken into use as "Stecca degli Artigiani" by craftspeople and associations, which transformed the adjacent grounds into parks. Then beginning in 2001, there were presentations of larger proposals for remodeling on the part of the right-wing city government. Here there was talk for the first time of a *City of Fashion* or *Città della Moda e del Design*, and the wording of the creative industries gradually spread. Offices, parking lots and a shopping center were to replace the Stecca and the parks. In 2005 the city turned over the major part of the Garibaldi Repubblica grounds, central to Isola, to the international real estate company *Hines* and the *Ligresti Group*.

Soft gentrification is based, not only in Isola, on multiple factors, such as a prepossessing rhetoric of participation and residents' involvement, soft ecological propaganda and the constant invocation of innovation and creativity. Investors purport to ensure everyone's participation in the planning. In fact, top-down processes are carried out here, steered by trained personnel and culminating in a divisive logic of inclusion and exclusion. Non-conformists are denounced as incapable of negotiating and are excluded; those who are included follow an increasing logic of subservience. Four levels can be differentiated in this process, although they largely overlap and merge with one another: repressive escalation, pseudo-participation as exclusion, activating participation and machinic subservience, co-deciding participation by elites.

The first level is a form of escalation, which tends to be avoided by and large, because it can generate undesirable images of repression. Nevertheless, in the case of Isola there was an example for repressive subjugation by the state apparatus and capitalist machine. Since the Stecca had attracted some international attention due to its transversal practice, the storming of the Stecca by police and Hines employees in 2007 had to be preceded by massive media campaigns against projects in the Stecca and on Isola as a whole, especially with the help of the classic hooks of drug dealing and criminality. Demolition of the building began immediately after the martial storming of it, to establish the private domination of the entire grounds by the real estate company once and for all.

The second level, often branded as "community building," is that of pseudo-participation. In larger meetings that were "open" to everyone, *Hines* set its propaganda machine in motion to achieve a consensus for the construction plans. Naturally, the plans centered around the human being ("l'uomo al centro" was one of the slogans of *Porta Nuova* in 2008, which is now what the entire project is called), but what does that mean concretely, and most of all: *which* human being? This level is especially cynical, because it dangles the carrot of having a stake in planning the future, but in fact, the pseudo-participating "stakeholders" are the group that is in danger of being driven out of their neighborhood by higher rents in the future.

The third level is that of participation as machinic subservience in the narrower sense. Civil society groups, associations and dedicated individuals are animated here to become an "active part" of the planning and realization process, participating in the process of transforming their own surroundings. This could also be called occupational therapy, where the well prepared representatives of the real estate multinational corporation define the terrain of the scope of action and especially the boundaries, within which smaller discussions can then be conducted about relatively trivial issues. These prior decisions about the boundaries of the discourse then also condition the division into good and evil, into the integration of the subservient and the exclusion of the indocile. The rhetoric function of participation is also evident at this level, but instead of resignation or rebellion, here it is a matter of active involvement in making the sociality of the quarter worse. On the side of involvement, the "good" groups that let themselves be taken into service (from architects to bicycle repairers, critical gardeners and green designers, all the way to environmentalist groups, most of them certainly with good intentions), may put up a brave front. They are promised accommodation in the end in a shiny "incubator," and for the transition phase they have to make do with the barracks provided by *Hines*.

It is only at the fourth level that participation occurs in the actual sense of the word, meaning taking part in decision-making about the most important issues of planning and development: in 2006 Studio Boeri—in the beginning on the side of the critics of the construction plans—was commissioned by *Hines* to carry out the planning for the grounds of the Stecca and the parks, the *Porta Nuova Isola*. At the same time, Stefano Boeri also took over the task of giving the project the ecological touch intended to attract the newly rich creative class. A "vertical forest," in other words a few little trees planted into the building, was to beautify one of the high-rise projects and provide expensive apartments under the label eco-quarter exactly in the previously public terrain of the old parks.

There is another line that permeates and reinforces all four levels of the rhetoric of participation: the invocation of innovation and creativity. This is entirely congruent with neoliberal urban development policies under the buzz word of the creative city, pushed by all possible right-wing, center-right, and center-left politicians throughout Europe and pseudo-scientifically supported by urban policy consulting experts like Richard Florida. Along this line of the creative city discourse, it is initially important that actors from the artistic field can be won for the gentrification projects. The intellectual and media capital of the local ex-documenta participant Boeri (who became city councilor for culture, fashion and design in Fall 2011) is invaluable in the development phase. The point of crystallization for this line is the concept of the incubator.

The proposal of turning the Stecca into an incubator had already come up in 2005. The "incubatore dell'Arte," an "incubator" of creativity, has also appeared since then in the discourse of the city planners. In recent years, the concept of the incubator has appeared more and more frequently as a mainly economically connoted development aspect of revitalization, representing the phase in which the creative chick is supposed to hatch. The most important quality of these kinds of incubators is the limitation to short-term use. In the interim use of buildings slated for renovation or demolition, as well as the time-limited use of new buildings by "creative" projects, primarily two things are insured: a constant turnover of the people involved, who do not interfere with economic and political interests due to their short-term involvement, but also an increase in the value of the quarter through ever new creative projects in the sense of a post-educated-middle class neo-bourgeoisie with a cultural affinity.

In this game, however, there are also the bad ones, those who do not take part, do not let themselves be taken into service, the indocile ones, the spoilsports, the ones who want no in-cubator either, but rather a *dirty cube* instead. In 2001, about the same time as the urban remodeling plans were made public in Isola, the *Isola Art Project* was founded. Although this was also an art project, it was one that had learned from the problems of earlier artistic uses of the factories. Parallel with other European projects, it was also in the midst of a new and rampant current of what was formerly called "political art" (and which it is increasingly called again now).

The focus here was no longer on the fetish of industrial ruins, nor on the pathos of the aesthetic act of individual artists, but rather on everyday life in Isola and, in particular, in the Stecca degli Artigiani with all the everyday problems, the diverse interests and social contexts of craftspeople, residents, drug users, artists, etc. For the latter, taking part in the transversal struggle against the transformation of the quarter could not work without a self-critical awareness of the function of art in processes of gentrification.

Against the background of local experiences from the past decades as well as against the backdrop of internationally known revitalization processes like SoHo, the mistakes and blind spots of these earlier years were not to be unreflectedly repeated.

An important effect of this new awareness was to not carry out a "pure" practice of art, nor a "pure" practice of organizing cultural events, of commercial crafts or of social work, but rather essentially a practice of polluting, soiling, contaminating. Under the name *Isola dell'Arte* and later *Isola Art Center*, the second floor of the Stecca was used from 2003 to 2007, where artists around their "sub-curator" Bert Theis invented the term *dirty cube*. Instead of filling the factory with installations, the buzz word site-specificity was taken quite literally here. The artistic works—partly permanently integrated in the rooms—were to serve the purpose, among others, of hindering eviction and the demolition of the Stecca. Along with this, cooperation with the residents was strengthened, including such practical assistance as art auctions to raise money for court costs in the many partially successful procedures of hindering and delaying the construction projects.

The *cube* is *dirty*, specifically because it is not to be regarded as an *incubator*, newly bringing art and capitalist economy together as smoothly as possible, but rather because it enables transversal concatenations of practices and groups that had not cooperated with one another before, and were now bringing disorder, impurity, disobedience into the worlds of Isola threatened by subservient deterritorialization.

Beyond the specific site-specificity of the *dirty cube*, and especially after eviction from the Stecca, the artist-activists developed a practice under the label *Isola Art Center* that they no longer call *site-specific*, but rather *fight-specific*. What happens in Isola is no longer solely an art practice, which includes and comments on the location of its positioning, but rather an art practice that gets involved in the specific fights relevant to this location. In the re-definition as "homeless art center," which has been organizing artistic practices and political events in businesses, bookshops, community centers and on shutters since 2007 in diaspora, in cooperation with the "Comitato I Mille" and the parents' association "Confalonieri," conjoined into the "Forum Isola," an industry of creativity is invented that is different from the one the real estate agents want to sell. Instead of the shiny promises of the *isola creativa*, what emerges here in the melee is the wild transversality of *isola industria*, which refuses obedience, cooperation and (self-) domestication in the incubators of the creative industry. With it, the new meaning of the term industry also takes form as driving busyness, overflowing industriousness, "industriosity."

6

ART STRIKE FOR ALL!

Gustav Metzger has always been famous for his very special projects. In 1959 he introduced the term "auto-destructive art" in his first manifesto and called it a "form of public art for industrial societies." In the early 1960s, he added the complementary term auto-creative art, an art of self-generating images and objects. By the mid-60s, his "liquid crystal projections" that grew out of these conceptual ideas were used for psychedelic shows of bands like Cream, The Who, The Move and others. In 1966 Metzger organized the highly regarded and influential symposium "DIAS— Destruction in Art Symposium" in London, in which not only the Viennese Actionists Hermann Nitsch, Günter Brus and Otto Mühl took part, but also Yoko Ono, Al Hansen, Jean-Jacques Lebel, Wolf Vostell and many others. Yet the climax of Metzger's relevance in art and political history was probably the attempt to break through the dialectic of *destruction* and *creation* entirely: for the exhibition "Art into Society—Society into Art" at the London Institute of Contemporary Arts (ICA) in 1974, he provided no object, neither an auto-creative nor an auto-destructive object, but instead only a written contribution for the exhibition catalogue. It centered around inciting himself and his artist colleagues to go on strike. In it, Gustav Metzger wrote:

> Throughout the entire twentieth century, artists have attacked the prevailing methods of production, distribution and consumption of art. These attacks on the organization of the art world have gained momentum in recent years. This struggle, aimed at the destruction of existing commercial and public marketing and patronage systems, can be brought to a successful conclusion in the course of the present decade.
>
> The refusal to labour is the chief weapon of workers fighting the system; artists can use the same weapon. To bring down the art system it is necessary to call for years without art, a period of three years—1977 to 1980—when artists will not produce work, sell work, permit work to go on exhibitions, and refuse collaboration with any part of the publicity machinery of the art world. This total withdrawal of labour is the most extreme collective challenge that artists can make to the state.

Cut to 30 years later.

In the midst of a live broadcast on a major French TV channel, there was a sudden intervention from a colorful troupe of activists. They interrupted the running casting show, using it as a platform for their own interests. They introduced themselves as Intermittents or Intermittents du spectacle, as people belonging to the group of cultural workers, who had enjoyed the privilege of the so-called "cultural exception" in France since the 1960s. The "exception culturelle" was the basis for cultural workers, who had no income in between two productions and who officially worked a certain number of hours over the whole year, to receive benefits from the unemployment funds.

From their perspective, the term Intermittents covers not only the core disciplines of art production, where interruptions are virtually the rule in their working conditions, but also all of the people working in the cultural field, or as they wrote themselves in a declaration in 2003, "participants in both art and industry":

> We are performers, interpreters, technicians. We are involved in the production of theater plays, dance and circus performances, concerts, records, documentary and feature films, TV shows, Reality-TV, the evening news and advertising. We are behind the camera and in front of it, on stage and backstage, we are on the street, in class-rooms, prisons and hospitals. The structures we work in range from non-profit projects to enter-tainment corporations listed on the stockmarket.

As participants in both art and industry, we are subject to a double flexibility: flexible working hours and flexible wages. The regulation on the insurance and unemployment of the Intermittents du spectacle originally arose from the need to secure a continuous income and cushion the discontinuity of employment situations. The regulation made it possible to flexibly arrange production and ensure the mobility of wage-dependent persons in between different projects, sectors and employments. [...] In an era when the utilization of labor is increasingly based on individuals bringing themselves into their work with all their subjective resources, and in which the space afforded to this subjectivity is increasingly limited and formatted, [our] struggle represents an act of resistance: we need to reappropriate the sense of our work at a personal and collective level."

Back to the particular intervention of the Intermittents in the casting show, which was only one specific variation of the Intermittents' resistance, along with striking larger festivals and spectacular protest actions, conducting militant research and organizing assemblies and demonstrations. For a few minutes there was confusion, heated discussions between the Intermittents and the moderator, who was forced to continue playing his moderating role live, despite his obvious reluctance; then the people responsible for the show came up with the obvious idea of inserting a long commercial break. In the video that the Intermittents produced and publicized themselves directly after the action, we also see what happened behind the scenes and during the commercial break: the activists were brutally beaten and thrown out by private security forces, so that the live broadcast with its exhibitionizing appropriation of everyday creativity could run its usual course.

In times of the subservience of desire, affect and cooperation, it becomes increasingly anachronistic to apply the old forms of resistance and demands from the striated spaces and times of industrialization, which provided reterritorializing responses to the industrial reterritorialization of work and life. The national union, the classic strike and traditional sabotage represent only segments in a spectrum of resistance that has necessarily become substantially broader. Yet the pure invocation of deterritorialization, nomadism, decentrality and dispersion is also insufficient to draw lines of flight from the present, diffuse assemblages of social subjugation and machinic subservience. More than ever before, current forms of resistance must carry out and renew both movements, that of reterritorialization and that of deterritorialization. They must newly streak and smooth the times, invent the other side of industry in a form of deterritorialization not to be made subservient, reterritorialize work and life in new ways.

Gustav Metzger's early intervention in the art economy and that of the Intermittents in the cultural industry exemplify the other side of industry: interruptions that invent new reterritorializations and new deterritorializations in their wild, inventive industriousness. Yet what does interrupting the time regimes mean, when exactly these same time regimes are based on governing through interruption, through modularization, through dispersing temporality? What does it mean to strike, when the continuity of the working day has been irrevocably relegated to the fordist past, even in Europe, just like the boundary between working time and leisure time? What can strike mean for the creative workers and industrialists, whose punch-clocks know no on and off, but only countless versions of on?

Except for a few, mostly outraged reactions immediately following its publication, Gustav Metzger's appeal to cease art production remained wholly futile. In contrast to the reenactment of the call for an art strike by a few Neoists in 1989, Metzger's appeal was not even discussed or considered for realization. Metzger conducted the three-year strike from 1977 to 1980 by himself. This probably had something to do with him being far ahead of his time and daring to enter previously unexplored territory.

In his appeal from 1974, Metzger explicitly referred to the traditional strike as the "chief weapon of workers fighting the system," and "exactly the same weapon" was now to be employed by artists. It seems then that Metzger wanted to transfer an old form of resistance inherited from industrial capitalism, undifferentiated and somewhat belated, to the art field. Similar to the way he understood his *auto-destructive art* as a "form of public art for industrial societies," he also invoked industrialization's forms of resistance. However, the art strike is not only a belated adaptation of the general strike to the art field, but in a certain way, it is also an early practice of refusal in the context of post-fordist modes of production. In the very field where the main components of this mode of production were anticipated, long before the post-fordist paradigm had prevailed as such, Metzger prefigured what a strike could look like in the smooth and newly striated times. He attempted to establish the refusal to work specifically in the art field, which is marked not only by extreme competitiveness, strong innovation pressure and an extreme diffusion of production locations, but also by the specific smoothness of its temporality. The time regime of artist production anticipated certain aspects of the seemingly self-determined modes of subjectivation that determine more and more social fields in post-fordism. In other words, proto-post-fordist conditions were found in the art field, and for this reason, the conditions also had to be given in precisely this art field, in order to develop the avant-garde of the post-fordist strike in the sense of the other side of industry.

In his call for a strike, Metzger already stated that the point was not simply that nothing should happen during the art strike: "In place of the practice of art, people can spend time on the numerous historical, esthetic and social issues facing art." With the help of strengthening theory in general and a critical analysis of society, a critical potential should be developed during the strike, in order to shift the terrain of art production itself. In the midst of refusing, of suspending, of striking production, Metzger wanted to invent a surplus that could not be taken directly into service again.

What do these goals of the art strike mean for the double necessity of new forms of deterritorialization and reterritorialization? Deterritorialization must relate here exactly to the interruption of the overall time regime, which is now deterritorialized in its entirety, not only to the time regime that governs labor and leisure as separate territories, but to that which covers the whole of life. And reterritorialization means newly streaking this entire time regime in a specific sense, namely in the sense of a self-determined use of time for relocating production itself, for shifting the industry of creativity, for concatenating the fragmented singularities. For Gustav Metzger, interrupting the whole of the time regime meant producing no art for three long years, but instead attempting to shift the terrain of his production. Three years is a long time, but necessary, because the molecular struggle for time is to be conducted in the pores of everyday life, the molecules of the whole of life, not just in passing.

Testing the interruption of the increasingly total post-fordist time regime particularly in a field that has always been distinguished by existing under the conditions of interruption and discontinuity is the central approach of the group that has made interruption itself their eponymous main concept. Ten years after the disastrous reform of the "exception culturelle," the Intermittents' struggles probably have to be objectively declared lost. Yet the many experiences of exchange about precarious modes of living and working, the militant investigations, the collective research work, the assemblies and actions, these are all a trove of experimental experiences that actualize Gustav Metzger's solitary proto-post-fordist endeavor, and which have streaked the smooth spaces and times of their subjects in a new way.

It was not a coincidence that the Intermittents chose the live broadcast of a casting show for their most spectacular appearance. As Horkheimer and Adorno already described in their attacks on the early developments of talent shows, the procedures of participating in audiovisual mass media are limited to organizing the "apocryphal field of amateurs" from the top down: the stage of the radio and of TV is the surface, on which pseudo-activation and machinic subservience are exercised and presented in an exemplary way, an apparatus that induces compliance and entices, leads and seduces consumers at the same time to actively adapt themselves. It goes straight to the heart of the machinic assemblage of subservience when the smooth time of this stage is perforated from the outside and interrupted, when a different, less smooth surface is revealed, that of the everyday work of the stagehands, scriptwriters, jingle designers: Intermittents.

If the subservient deterritorialization of time is accompanied by the fragmentation and particularization of the whole of time, the Intermittents used the "privilege" of the "cultural exception" over the course of decades to try out a self-chosen form of smooth time. Consequent to the attacks on these free spaces from the side of neoliberal social policies, they also began to fill the interrupted time with the new, industrious industry of their strikes, interventions and actions.

Intermittence means not only precarious existence in the smooth in-between of the cultural field, but also a chain of deterritorializing and reterritorializing ruptures in the total temporality, in which regular behavior no longer exists, but only a hierarchized continuity of discontinuity. Intermittence is the interruption of the interruption and, at the same time, an industrious filling of interrupted time. Just as Gustav Metzger's art strike linked deterritorializing components of refusal with the reterritorializing components of relocating production, the struggles of the Intermittents involve a double movement of smoothing and newly streaking their temporality.

Yet the model of the "cultural exception" only takes effect as an industry of a new kind, when it is no longer claimed in the sense of a professional privilege, but rather when the social protection of the precarious in the cultural field is taken as an example for *all* the precarious, and when their own, initially limited privileges are transversalized into a more general struggle for social rights. New, appropriate forms of interruption have to be found here again and again, both at the level of the event, the temporary rupture of smooth time, and at the level of duration, which provides the fundamental possibilities of using all the "cultural exceptions" that the art field has to offer for a wild reappropriation of time, and to turn this non-subservient industry into an example for other fields and transversalize it.

7

FOR A MOLECULAR ACTIVISM

17 September 2011. A demonstration march
through lower Manhattan chooses as the destination
of its dérive a small park near the enormous construction site of the World Trade Center. Zuccotti
Park is a formerly public, now privatized square
belonging to the real estate corporation Brookfield
Properties, named after its chairman John Zuccotti.
On older maps of the financial district, however, this
square has a different name: Liberty Plaza. The
demonstrators have not chosen to occupy this territory because of a universalist invocation of freedom,
but rather because they want to set a further component of the abstract machine in motion that has
drawn lines of flight throughout the entire year,
especially through the Mediterranean region. And
the most intensive line of this abstract machine was
probably the Egyptian part of the Arab Spring with
its center in Tahrir Square, the "Place of Freedom."
By purposely occupying another place of freedom at
the edge of Wall Street, the precarious occupiers seek
not only to interrupt subservient deterritorialization,

the flows through the global financial center, but they also take up the practices, with which current activisms de- and re-territorialize their times, their socialities, their lives in new ways.

In his last course with the title "The Courage of Truth," Michel Foucault explored the scandalous life of the Cynics, to which he applied the colorful term of "philosophical activism." It was not his intention to attribute a privileged position to the activity of the philosophers, even less to reduce activism to a cognitive capacity. Rather, the Cynic philosopher served as a backdrop for a more general form of activism, of changing the world, of newly inventing worlds. For Foucault in later years, philosophical activism was an "activism in the world and against the world."

The Cynic philosopher is, first of all, the exemplary, anecdotal, almost mythical figure of Diogenes, with no permanent residence, at most a tub, living his life completely in public, scandalously all the way to masturbating in public, practicing *parrhesia*, the manner of "saying everything," even if it is associated with great risk, which in Cynicism conjoins the art of existence with the discourse of truth. Foucault's endeavor of a "history of life as possible beauty" situates this old Greek Cynicism as the pivotal point of a whole genealogy of scandalous, disobedient, self-forming forms of living. Foucault sees historical actualizations of Cynic activism in the minoritarian heretical movements of the Middle Ages, in the political revolutions of modernity, and—somewhat surprisingly—in the theme of the artist's life in the nineteenth century. And here I would add to the Foucaultian genealogy the new activisms of the twenty-first century: anti-globalization movement, social forums, anti-racist no border camps, queer-feminist activisms, transnational migrant strikes, Mayday movements of the precarious. Now since last year there has been a tremendous intensification of these new activisms in the wider Mediterranean region: from the waves of university occupations to the revolutions of the Arab Spring, all the way to the movements of occupying central squares in Greece, Spain and Israel. Day-long sit-ins at the Kasbah Square in Tunis, revolutionary occupations of Tahrir Square in Cairo, Acampadas in the Puerta del Sol in Madrid, tents in the Rothschild Boulevard in Tel Aviv. Much could be said about what these new activisms have in common. They are all about appropriating real places, about a struggle against precarization, against extreme competition and against the drivenness of contemporary production, largely dispensing with representation and weaving a transnational concatenation of social movements. There are, however, three specific vectors, on which these activisms enter new territory: in their search for new forms of living, in their organizational forms of radical inclusion, and in their insistence on re-appropriating time.

Inventing New Forms of Living

When Foucault brings art into play, following the revolutions in his genealogy of the Cynics, it is not classical aesthetics or an existentialist theory of art that concerns him, but rather art that is "capable of giving a form to existence which breaks with every other form," a form that forms itself, newly invents itself, an "aesthetics of existence." Aesthetics as ethics, as the invention of new modes of subjectivation and of new forms of living (together), existence as aesthetic object, life as a beautiful work. This ethico-aesthetic aspect of forming life is by no means to be understood as an individualistic stylization of life: even though dandyism and existentialism certainly also belong to the genealogy of the aesthetics of existence, the term does not refer to an aesthetization of the artist's existence. Instead, Foucault's examples go in the direction of relationship, of exchange, and not in the direction of the pure and autonomous implementation of a self-relation. Forming life as living together takes place at the microphysical and the macrophysical level, in the forming of the individual body, in the forming of social relations. In his lecture, Foucault explicitly says about this: "By basing the analysis of Cynicism on this theme of individualism, however, we are in danger of missing what from my point of view is one [of its] fundamental dimensions, that is to say, the problem, which is at the core of Cynicism, of establishing a relationship between forms of existence and manifestation of the truth." Philosophical activism is not about a model philosophical or artistic life beyond relations, at the edge of the world. Cynics live in the midst of the world, against the world, with the horizon of an other world; in Foucault's words, they have "laid down this otherness of an *other* life, not simply as the choice of a different, happy, and sovereign life, but as the practice of an activism on the horizon of which is an *other* world."

This understanding of an other life enabling an other world applies all the more to the collective Cynicism, or rather: the molecular Cynicism of the new activisms today. In this kind of molecular Cynicism, it is not the individual philosopher, not the dandyesque artist, not the existentialist activist that is at the center, but rather the exchange relations of singularities testing disobedient, non-subservient, industrious forms of living.

If today's revolutions are not only taken as molar, as—in a narrow sense—political projects, but rather also as molecular revolutions, then the aesthetics of existence takes its place alongside the political project as a "continual and constantly renewed work of giving form [to life]," to living together. A contemporary concept of molecular revolution requires the ethico-aesthetic level of transforming forms of living into a beautiful and good life, as well as the becoming of forms of living together across continents: micro-machines, which in their singular situativity develop disobedient modes of existence and subjectivation, as well as translocally dispersed, global abstract machines. The molecular revolution also comprises the "ethical revolution" that is called for at the end of the manifesto of the Spanish occupiers of M-15. The multitude that occupied the many main squares of Spain beginning on 15 May 2011 for several weeks is not particularly interested in gaining symbolic space and media attention. The occupiers take over the occupied squares, they appropriate them and make them their own, even though they know they are only there for a certain time. This time, however, is decisive, an extraordinarily important time of their lives, the time of assemblies and the social time of living together, of residing and sleeping in the occupied squares. Their new ethico-aesthetic paradigm seeks revolution in the forming of their own lives and of living together. The call for an ethical revolution is thus not at all a kind of first demand for different, better politicians, nor simply the obvious demand that corrupt politics should resign as a whole. Instead, it is a demand to themselves, a call for fundamental transformations, for the fabrication of non-subservient machinic modes of living, for disobedient industries, for non-conforming forms of living together.

Inventing New Forms of Organization

When today's activisms turn against a one-sidedly molar procedure, this does not mean that they neglect aspects of organization and reterritorialization. Yet the streaking of time and space finds its own molecular procedures. Molecular modes of organization are not organic, but rather orgic-industrious, not centered around representation, but non-representationist, not hierarchically differentiating, but radically inclusive. Molecularity does not focus on taking over state power, but it takes effect in the pores of everyday life, in the molecules of forms of living. Molar organization arises as striating reterritorialization, it focuses struggles on an essence, a main contradiction, a master. In a molecular world of dispersion and multiplicity, a different form of reterritorialization is needed, inclusive and transversal, beyond individual or collective privileges. Transversality means that the movements of reterritorialization and deterritorialization do not pursue particular goals, they do not establish and secure privileges. Instead they smooth and streak territories by crossing through them. The special rights of every single singularity are diametrically opposed to all individual or collective privileges. Yet these special rights only exist where every singularity can fully live its own specialness, try out its own form of concatenation, streak its own time. There is no privileged position for the intellectuals, for art or activism. Exclusivity for all. Molecular struggles are struggles that emerge accidentally and spread further through what is accidental to the accidentals. No master heads the molecular organization.

The Cynic philosopher is an anti-king. Philosophical activism is not practiced in the form of sects, communities, in the form of small numbers. Instead, there is no community at all in Cynicism; the Cynic form of philosophical activism is, according to Foucault, "in the open, as it were, that is to say, an activism addressed to absolutely everyone." This kind of openness evolves in the practice of the new molecular activisms. In the language of the activists it places radical inclusion at the center of assemblies, discussions and actions. An "activism addressed to absolutely everyone," and yet nevertheless not operating universalistically, but transversally, like the tent camp in the Rothschild Boulevard in Tel Aviv, for example, following which the largest demonstration for social justice in the history of Israel took place in early September 2011. Radical inclusion means here, most of all, establishing an open milieu, in which the right to a place to live is not only demanded for everyone, but also acted out straight away in protest. The tent assemblages, the assemblies, the discussions are already living examples of the radical inclusion and transversality of the movement.

In the case of #occupy wallstreet, the tendency to radical inclusion is evident primarily in the invention and development of general assemblies. These are not so much "general assemblies" in the conventional sense, but rather transversal assemblages of singularities, which renew the grassroots-democratic experiences of the anti-globalization and social forums movement, further developing them into a form of polyvocality—for instance in the invention, almost by chance and out of necessity, of a new procedure of "amplification": because the police forbid them to use microphones, megaphones or other technical means, they began to repeat every single sentence from the speakers in chorus. The functionality of this repetition consists, first of all, in making the speech intelligible for hundreds of people in an open air setting. Yet the chorus as amplification here is neither a purely neutral medium of conveyance nor a euphoric affirmation of the speakers. It can happen that the chorus, whose voice is speaking the same thing, proves to be radically polyvocal and differentiated: one voice supports the speaker with hand signs, the next, while repeating the sentence, declares dissent with other hand signs, and the third has turned away from the speaker to better ensure the amplifying function for the others listening. Even though this new practice is called the "people's mic," it is not at all homogenizing, does not lead to a unanimity of the multitude. No main issue is formed from the many incidental issues, no one and nothing is made an exception. The mic amplification supports the singularities and the different forms of organization, concatenation, reterritorialization.

Industrious Reappropriation of Time

Just as the Cynic philosopher seeks scandal in the offensive transparency of his life, the new activisms speak clearly by taking the empty promise of "public space" at its word. This is the exercise, as widely visible as possible, of deviant modes of subjectivation, not or not only in the nakedness, placelessness and promiscuity of the Cynics, but most of all in playing with the paradox of the public: public space does not exist, and most of all not in the smooth spaces of urban centers, whether they are the touristic non-places of the Puerta del Sol or the Rothschild Boulevard, whether it is the privatized sphere of Zuccotti Park, or whether it is the heavy traffic of Tahrir Square. And yet, or specifically because of this, the new activisms occupy the central squares, turn them into common-places, as a paradoxical provocation of normativity and normalization. And beyond this spatial re-territorialization, it is primarily the re-appropriation of time that marks the protestors' modes of action. In the midst of the hectic drivenness of Wall Street, the traffic in Tahrir Square, the tourism industry of the Spanish capitals, they develop a new drive, a different manner of traffic, an inventive industry. In the midst of the nervous poly-rhythms of precarious life, in its mixture of drivenness and melancholy, they invent a surplus. In all that subservience they create a desire to not be taken into service in that way. In the midst of hurried timelessness, the precarious strikers insist on different time-relations; they streak the time in the patience of assemblies, in spreading out living, residing, sleeping in the squares, feeling their way to the first rudimentary possibilities of a new form of resistance, the molecular strike.

The occupiers take the space and time seriously that they set up, striate, streak, taking time for long, patient discussions and taking time to stay in this place, developing a new everyday life, even if only for a short time. The Asambleas, General Assemblies and People's Mics are not only forms of polyvocity, of the expansion of the multitude to its many voices, they are also modes of subjectivation of gaining time. Gaining time, at the same time springing out of subserviently smoothed time, that is the practice of industrious creativity. The new, disobedient industry of creativity does not aim to monopolize the time gain, seeks to make no exception, introduce no privileges. Industriosity is instead the monstrous form that is suitable for virally expanding the experience of gaining time. Beyond activist practice, it is also capable of developing duration and a self-determined streaking of time, where there was otherwise only timeless smoothness and striating interruption.

In an otherwise boundless everyday life, the molecular strike spreads out these small new durations and streakings. Its institution, however, first requires an evental break with subservient deterritorialization in machinic capitalism. The molecular strike is both: duration and break. It is not leaving, not dropping out of this world, no time-out. The molecular strike is the breach in the time regime of subservient deterritorialization that we drive in, in order to try out new ways of living, new forms of organization, new time relations. It is no longer a struggle merely to reduce working time, but rather for an entirely new streaking of time as a whole. In machinic capitalism, it is a matter of the whole, the totality of time, its entire appropriation. The molecular strike struggles for its reappropriation, its streaking, piece by piece. The new Wobblies will be no Industrial Workers of the World, but rather Industrious Workers of the world, a gigantic industry carrying everything along with it, not submitting to subservient deterritorialization, at the same time a reterritorialization, an industrious refrain, a dangerous class that will no longer let its time be stolen.

Afterword by Antonio Negri

COUNTERMELODY

There is no need to insist on the depth and efficacy of Gerald Raunig's research. It represents a passage that, while fully assuming the horizon of capital's real subsumption of society and the totalitarian capture of use value by exchange value, pushes us beyond the sad passions of the Frankfurt's School, frees us from reading "weak postmodernist thought" and mocks any linear figure of subsumption, even when clad in Situationist irony. Raunig's texts move across the area spanning from Deleuze and Guattari's *A Thousand Plateaus* to post-workerist constitutions, producing rich and articulate modulations on the critique of power and inaugurating new lines of flight, desertions, the dialectics of new worlds and creative reterritorializations. This countermelody runs against all those developments of postmodern thought (but also of post-workerism) that congeal otherwise open lines of critique, and read moments of resistance in a rigid and excessively theoretical manner. It is an essential countermelody, which brings us all back to Earth.

But maybe we do need a countermelody to the nth power. In other words, issues are brought to the fore, and from Raunig's conclusions we need to elaborate other practical, constructive and political hypotheses. This is our second chance: Raunig's book showed us another world, another narration needs to begin at the point when he stopped (to take a Kafkian metaphor: we need a new "Josephine" singing to a "reformed" people of mice). Giacomo Leopardi, in his splendid Batrachomiomachy, had already seen a movement, a displacement within the mouse world, although still at the level of individual, heroic passions. For Raunig, instead, these movements are plural, they belong to the multitude and the free singularities that constitute it. What is the issue, then, that a newly created melody can address for a second time? It is the overcoming of the refrain, of the alternative between a smooth and striated space, of territorialization and deterritorialization. Raunig—and Josephine—have irrevocably brought us on the space of politics: *Hic Rhodus, hic salta.*

These are not the problems of those who want to found yet another party, but of the subversives who think about how to organize the multitude, how to have singularities meet in the soviets, in the councils of manual and intellectual laborers finally able to reclaim their common life. The relation between singularity and multitude can in fact be articulated, at least in part, in terms of deterritorialization and reterritorialization. Today, moreover, we see a point of verticality, a sharp inner intensity, a quasi-solar condensation causing effects of attraction and resistance on a network of forces yet to be discovered. A "place."

I recall long discussions with Félix Guattari precisely on this issue: what "machinic" point of productive interference, what new *agencement* can constitute a local expressive function within a field of immanence that multiplies segments and unstoppable velocities? In those years, our two masters were finishing their work on Kafka, and already in that essay the answer was that the machine could only be localized as the consistency and coexistence of intensive qualities. In a translation accessible to the uninitiated that I was, this meant to seize—in the field of immanence constituted by class struggles—the intensive quantities of the material tendency of capital toward its own crisis together with those constituting the resource for the workers' refusal of exploitation and the revolutionary energy that was active then with an intense, higher desire for a communism consistent with the present space of crisis and struggle. This energy was minoritarian, it's true, but we know that minorities make up in intensity what they lack in number. A powerful, sweeping energy creating a "space." About fifteen years later, Deleuze answered my question about the specificity of communist class struggle affirming that the system of lines of flight defining capitalism could only be countered with the construction of a "war machine." This means that we need to determine a localized space-time, a constituent power and a capacity to resist for a people yet-to-come. Another "space" then, not static but creative, that is essential for this countermelody to the nth power.

The actions of *Occupy* and the *acampadas* of the *indignados* push us to work on the definition of this verticality, this intensity, this place. It is no longer an issue of pure temporality. Benjamin recalled how the workers, during the insurrections of the 19th century, used to shoot the clocks in the city squares, denouncing in the measuring of time the mechanism of their exploitation. Now, in their rebellion, the precarious workers need to shoot the calendars—which mark the separation, and not the continuity, of time, the succession of the distinct times of capitalist valorization—since their exploitation, their alienation, are mostly measured in spatial mobility, in the separation of their workplaces, in local contiguity and cooperation and in the diversity of the spaces they have to inhabit. Like the migrants, the precarious worker is constantly looking for a place to rest. Without this place, it is impossible to revolt. But is this true, or is this affirmation a simple mark of frustration? Anyway, this is the question that led us to Zuccotti Park, the square of freedom. The movements, then, need to be reformed around a space—a verticality crosses them, localizing and elevating them with extreme punctual intensity.

This is the countermelody to the nth power that I am appending to Raunig's, against certain postworkerist rigidities. This melody brings us back to the struggle for a reclamation of common life, for a revolutionary engagement for the transformation of money in an ubiquitous and transversal currency for everyday use, for the productive utopia of a common institution organized in a democratic and participatory manner. We have walked for a long time, living formidable adventures: now we need to rest for a while, in a place, because only in a place can we continuously renew Josephine's song.

—*Translated by Giuseppina Mecchia*

References

Bertolt Brecht, "Das Badener Lehrstück vom Einverständnis," in: ibid., *Gesammelte Werke 2*, Frankfurt/Main: Suhrkamp 1967, 601: "7. Die Verlesung der Kommentartexte."

Gilles Deleuze, "Postscript on Control Societies," in: ibid., *Negotiations. 1972–1990*, New York: Columbia 1995, 177–182.

Gilles Deleuze, Félix Guattari, *A Thousand Plateaus*, translation and forward by Brian Massumi, Minneapolis/London: University of Minnesota Press 1987.

edu-factory, *L'università globale: il nuovo mercato del sapere*, Rome: manifestolibri 2008.

Michel Foucault, "The Political Function of the Intellectual," trans. Colin Gordon, *Radical Philosophy* 17, 1977.

Michel Foucault, *The Courage of Truth*, edited by Frédéric Gros, translated by Graham Burchell, Palgrave Macmillan 2011.

GlobalProject/Coordination des Intermittents et Précaires d'Ile de France, "Spectacle Inside the State and Out. Social Rights and the Appropriation of Public Spaces: The Battles of the French Intermittents," http://eipcp.net/transversal/0704/intermittents/en

Justin Hoffmann, Gustav Metzger, "Die Erfindung des Art Strike. Gustav Metzger im Interview mit Justin Hoffmann," http://www.iamthemotherofpearl.org/writings/articles/hilfe_archive/Hilfe4/art.htm

Max Horkheimer, Theodor W. Adorno, *Dialectic of Enlightenment. Philosophical Fragments*, trans. Edmund Jephcott, Stanford: Stanford University Press 2002.

Franz Kafka, "Josephine the Singer, or The Mouse Folk," in: ibid., *Selected Short Stories of Franz Kafka*, translated by Willa and Edwin Muir, Random House 1952, 304–328.

"Manifiesto Movimiento 15M—Democracia Real YA!," http://movimiento15m.org/manifiesto-movimiento-15m-%C2%A1democracia-real-ya/

Karl Marx, *Capital*, Volume One, http://www.marxists.org/archive/marx/works/1867-c1/

Karl Marx, *Economic Manuscripts: Grundrisse*, p. 702–750: http://www.marxists.org/archive/marx/works/1857/grundrisse/ch14.htm

Gustav Metzger, "Art Strike 1977–1980," http://www.thing.de/projekte/7:9%23/y_Metzger+s_Art_Strike.html

Gerald Raunig, *A Thousand Machines. A Concise Philosophy of the Machine as Social Movement*, translated by Aileen Derieg, Los Angeles/New York: Semiotext(e) 2010.

Heinz Steinert, Hubert Treiber, *Die Fabrikation des zuverlässigen Menschen. Über die "Wahlverwandtschaft" von Kloster-und Fabriksdisziplin*. Munich: Moos 1980.

Paolo Virno, *Grammar of the Multitude*, translated by Isabella Bertoletti, James Cascaito, Andrea Casson, Los Angeles/New York: Semiotext(e) 2004.

Wolf Wagner, *Uni-Angst und Uni-Bluff*, Berlin: Rotbuch 1977.

"The Occupation Cookbook, or the Model of the Occupation of the Faculty of Humanities and Social Sciences in Zagreb 2009," http://www.scribd.com/doc/50823076/

Acknowledgements

Thanks to Isabell Lorey, Aileen Derieg, Marcelo Expósito, Michael Heitz und Sabine Schulz, Jens Kastner, Therese Kaufmann, Hedi El Kholti, Maurizio Lazzarato, Sylvère Lotringer, Victoria Lynn, Sandro Mezzadra, Raimund Minichbauer, Gianfranco Morosato, Toni Negri, Brett Neilson, Roberto Nigro, Stefan Nowotny, Nikos Papastergiadis, Otto Penz, Raúl Sanchez, Birgit Sauer, Klaus Schönberger, Ruth Sonderegger, Bert Theis, Nato Thompson, Irene Vögeli, Dan S. Wang.

Thanks also to the students and teachers of the Department for Arts and Media at the Zürcher Hochschule der Künste, the Faculty for Radical Aesthetics, the European Institute for Progressive Cultural Policies (eipcp) and edu-factory.